CELEBRITY
Vegetarian
COOKBOOK

Edited by Geoff Francis & Janet Hunt

GREEN
PRINT

Green Print
Marshall Pickering
3 Beggarwood Lane, Basingstoke, Hants RG23 7LP, UK

First published in 1988 by Green Print
Part of the Marshall Pickering Holdings Group
A subsidiary of the Zondervan Corporation

ISBN 1 85425 017 5

Personality portraits by **Dr Brian Hinton** and **Geoff Francis**
Food Editor and Advisor **Janet Hunt**
Designed by **Lawrence & Beavan**
Illustrated by **Lesley Champkins**
Typeset by **Windhorse**
Printed by **Purnell**, Bristol

Thanks to Cath and Ian Fletcher for hours of patient wordprocessing.

Preface

As the planning of this book reached its final stages, and we began to compile the biographies of those who had taken part, an interesting pattern seemed to emerge. Not only the obvious one of people knowing each other and even working together, but a deeper underlying motif; what our contributors share is drive and commitment, the ability to use their talents in causes greater than themselves.

Concern about animals, starvation in the Third World, and the survival of this planet does not stop when you achieve fame. This book just goes to prove the point.

On the following pages, you will find a wide selection of favourite recipes contributed by people whose careers may be glamorous, but who are still forthright about their principles. They support us in spreading the message that eating meat not only deprives animals of life, but humans too, and will eventually cost the earth.

All the contributors have given their time and effort free, in order to help feed malnourished children. We thank them for their help. You too will have helped by buying this book.

By using the book, you will help even more.

Geoff Francis
Ryde, 1988

Contents

Soups

Snacks & Starters

Pasta

Salads

Main Meals

Sweets & Baked Things

But from the mountain's grassy side,
A guiltless feast I bring,
A scrip with herbs and fruit supplied,
And water from the spring.

OLIVER GOLDSMITH

It has been estimated that every minute eighteen children and six adults die from malnutrition. Yet according to well-respected sources there is more than enough food to feed the world's population. So what happens? Where does the food go?

The answer is that much food, which could be used for direct human consumption, or is grown on land which could be used to feed humans, is in fact being fed to animals – not for any altruistic purpose, but to satisfy an appetite: the appetite for meat.

Meat is a rich man's food which is costing the planet and its disadvantaged inhabitants their lives. More than half the world's grain, one third of the world's milk production, and half the world's sea catch is fed to animals. Yet, in terms of pure economics, animals waste food: it can take as much as 22 lbs of vegetable protein to yield 1 lb of meat when fed to beef cattle.

The way we eat is something we can all control. By changing our diet we can affect the market place which gives an imprisoned battery animal greater purchasing power than a malnourished child in the Third World. If Africa were allowed to keep the food it produces it could provide 1,700 calories per person. Britain, because of its heavy reliance on meat, actually produces only 1,666 calories per person. But the average person's daily requirement is 3,000 calories. This requires that we rely heavily on imports, many of which come from Third World sources.

In 1984, for instance, when the nation's TV screens and hearts were concentrated on Ethiopia, our farmers imported £1.5 million of grain from that country to feed to animals. Even when we, as individuals, have decided to avoid plundering the world for our dinner plates, there are still the basic questions which need to be asked about our approach to aid.

Some aid is uncompromisingly imperialistic: "food as a weapon". Some is aimed at creating new markets: wheat-eating battery hens, hamburgers, and agribusiness. Some is

Our task must be to free ourselves ... by widening our circle of compassion to embrace all living creatures and the whole of nature in its beauty.

ALBERT EINSTEIN

fired with religious zeal and has an accompanying price tag. Nearly all aid entails an unwitting arrogance which sees the Western lifestyle as a model to be emulated.

Happily there is an increasing number of projects where the indigenous population is dealing with the problems by the appropriate application of local resources, without doing violence to local culture and ecology.

One such organisation is Sarvodaya Shramadana in Sri Lanka. Sarva means 'all', Udaya means 'well-being' and within the word are understood the concepts of self-development, self-fulfilment, self-reliance, self-realization and non-dependence. This was the basis of a movement conceived in India by Gandhi in the 1920s. It is based on the Buddhist principles of truth and non-violence and introduced a unique approach to community and national development. The idea was fittingly transferred to Sri Lanka in the 1970s by a young doctor teaching at Ariyaratne. Today nearly 20% of the popularion are involved. Sarvodaya seeks a total transformation of society using the tools of spiritual awakening and personal growth, teachings inherited in the country's Buddhist and Hindu heritage.

The greatness of a nation and its moral progress can be judged by the way its animals are treated.

The world holds enough for every man's need but not for every man's greed.

MOHANDAS GANDHI

The royalties from this book will be going to extend work in one of their projects, which is providing leaf protein for pre-school children. Kola Kanda is a food which has been used and revered in Sri Lanka for centuries. For the Westerner it is best described as a porridge made with ground rice, coconut and leaf juice. The juice contains proteins, vitamins and minerals which fortify the porridge.

Traditionally, leaves were pounded in a mortar and pestle. To cut production time and increase the quantities, a manual pulping machine was designed with the help of Find Your Feet – a British charity working exclusively on leaf protein – and built from scrap and local materials. The machine ruptures the leaf cells to release the proteins. In contrast to traditional methods the juice extracted is then boiled until it curdles. This curd nutritionally resembles milk. The curds are separated and from the whey by filtering and then added to porridge. One tablespoon of curd gives a growing child one third of its protein needs, plus its Vitamin A. On a dry weight basis the curd contains 55% protein of a quality higher even than soya. It is also a valuable source of iron, calcium and beta carotene which the body turns to Vitamin A.

We chose this project because it is one which has been instigated by the people themselves. It extends the use of a traditional food source and at the same time does no violence to local beliefs and understanding. It is equally important that it does no violence to other creatures. It is a totally vegetarian and ecologically sound process. The waste pulp is used for mulch.

Through the sponsored 'Wot! No Meat?' weeks and with like-minded organisations such as Animal Aid, Compassion in World Farming, The Vegan Society and The Vegetarian Society as part of the 'Great British Meat Out', Enough has so far raised several thousand pounds for this project. We hope this book will serve to raise more.

As an exciting footnote, the people from Sarvodaya have recently demonstrated a machine in the Philippines, where it is being copied for use.

Animals are my friends … and I don't eat my friends.

GEORGE BERNARD SHAW

HOW TO USE THIS BOOK

If the idea of planning and preparing meals without using animal-derived ingredients is completely new to you, you may at first find it rather strange to base your meals on vegetables, grains, nuts, pulses and dairy produce. You may worry that you are going to be missing out on flavour, nutrients, or whatever.

Have no fear!

Though the fast growing interest in this way of eating seems to be something recent, vegetarian cookery has been around for centuries – in fact, the majority of the world's population even today will never or only rarely eat meat. Numerous books give instructions on cooking techniques ranging from the simple stir-fry (so popular in the Far East) to exotic curries. Most cities have outlets where you can buy fresh spices, woks, bean sprouters, couscoussiers – whatever it is you need to either feed your family, or enhance your reputation as a Cordon Vert cook! If you have the desire to learn, to experiment, there is nothing to stop you.

First, though, it's best to master some of the simpler dishes. Many of them you'll already be familiar with – few people eat meat at every meal, after all. The recipes in this book will give you plenty of ideas. Look through it, pick out one or two dishes that especially appeal, and have a go. As with all types of cookery, it's probably best to follow the instructions as closely as possible when you first try a dish, though with experience you'll find you can vary the ingredients to suit your tastes (and what's in your cupboard!). Once you've got the idea, try more dishes. Or combine two or three to make a complete meal when you're entertaining.

QUANTITIES

Because each of our contributors has a different approach to cookery, each recipe is different. Some, for example, will feed one – others will feed a party of ten or more! Adapt the quantities to suit yourself, taking into consideration what you intend to serve with a dish. A vegetable recipe such as Courgettes Niçoises could be a small starter for four, or could be served as an accompaniment to something like a nut roast.

Alternatively, topped with cheese or nuts for extra protein, and served with rice or jacket potatoes, it could make a main meal for two.

Appetites do, of course, vary considerably so that a main meal for two might make no more than a tasty snack for someone else! As a general guide, though, consider that 2–3 oz (55–85g) of pasta make one serving. The same is true for most grains, such as rice. When making soup, a normal serving for one is ⅓–½ pint (200–285ml). Beans, being much more filling, are best served in small quantities – say 2 oz (55g) per person. When combined with vegetables and/or grains they make a very satisfying and nutritious dish. When using tofu, allow approximately 5 oz (140g) for each person.

GOING VEGAN

Dairy produce – in the western world at least – involves a good deal of cruelty to animals and wasteful use of resources, so you might feel you want to reduce your consumption. Nowadays this is easier than ever, with manufacturers producing various soya-based alternatives to many of the foods we use most often: milk, yogurt, mayonnaise, ice cream, and so on. Look out for them in your local wholefood and healthfood shops, and in supermarkets and chemists too. If you don't find them, ask. No shopkeepers will want to miss out on sales so if you make it clear there's a demand, they'll surely want to satisfy it. One warning: though you'll hardly notice the difference in cooked dishes, many of these 'substitute' ingredients don't taste exactly like the originals. Don't expect them to. Think of them as something completely different and enjoy them for what they are – delicious, nutritious, and completely free from any association with animals!

Maybe one of the most important things about cooking without meat – true, also, of so many things you do in life – is to enjoy it. The celebrities who contributed these recipes enjoy both preparing and eating them, so here's your chance to follow in their footsteps.

Bon appétit!

I must interpret the life about me as I interpret the life that is my own. My life is full of meaning to me. The life around me must be full of significance to itself.

DR ALBERT SCHWEITZER

SOUPS

Paul and Linda McCartney

GREEN PEA SOUP

¾ lb (340g) green split peas, soaked in water overnight, then drained
½ lb (227g) orange lentils
1 large onion, quartered
¼ cleaned head of celery, including leaves, chopped
2 peeled tomatoes, chopped
2 leeks, cleaned and chopped
(plus any suitable leftover vegetables)
1-2 oz (30-55g) butter or margarine
Seasoning to taste

Combine all the ingredients in a large saucepan and just cover with water, then add approximately 1½ pints more water.

Bring to the boil, then cover the pan, lower the heat, and simmer the mixture until everything is cooked. This could take anything from one to three hours.

When ready to serve, stir in butter or margarine and flavour generously with salt and freshly ground black pepper.

After studying art at the University of Arizona, Linda McCartney moved to New York, where her photographs of rock stars of the Woodstock generation quickly established her reputation among the counter-culture of the time. Her images have been described as 'intimate, reticent and without fuss', a woman's viewpoint which gently cuts down to size some of the overblown egos of that era, while celebrating family life and the transience of the moment. It was while on a photographic assignment in London that Linda met and subsequently married Paul McCartney; she later played keyboards in his post-Beatles group 'Wings' as well as exhibiting her work in London, Paris and New York. Linda is a co-founder of Animaline.

Perhaps the most famous pop musician in the world, Paul McCartney also has a keen interest in a compassionate diet. On his farm in Sussex, the animals actually live out their full span without any requirements being made of them.

Sophie Ward is one of Britain's brightest young actresses. Her first starring role was in Steven Spielberg's 'Adventures of Young Sherlock Holmes', since when she has appeared in several major films. A vegetarian, Sophie has been generous with her time in promoting the animals' cause, notably in her support for the Choose Cruelty-Free campaign for non-animal-tested cosmetics.

Sophie Ward

LENTIL & LEMON SOUP

1 cup orange lentils
3 teaspoons walnut oil
2 small onions, finely chopped
2 teaspoons Vecon
1½ pints water
2-3 teaspoons crushed coriander seeds
Juice and rind of 1½ lemons
Black pepper

CROUTONS:
2 tablespoons vegetable oil
2 slices granary bread, cut into 1½" squares
2 cloves garlic, crushed

Simmer the lentils in three cups of water for 30 minutes, then strain.

Heat the walnut oil in a large saucepan, and sauté the finely chopped onions until browned.

Make a stock with 1½ pints water and two teaspoons of Vecon, and add this and the cooked lentils to the onions. Sprinkle in the coriander seeds, and season with a good twist of black pepper. Allow to simmer for 30 minutes.

Add the lemon juice and finely grated rind.

Serve with croutons: heat the oil and garlic in a frying pan, then add in the bread; cook until crisp and golden. The garlic flavours the oil and will be left in the pan when the croutons are ready.

Serves 4.

Francis Wilson

FRENCH ONION SOUP

1 small onion, sliced
2 teaspoons corn oil
2 teaspoons flour
½ pint (285ml) vegetable stock
Salt
Freshly ground black pepper
1 tablespoon chopped parsley
1 thick slice French bread
2 tablespoons grated Parmesan cheese

Fry onion in oil for about 4 minutes to brown. Stir in flour and stock. Season and add parsley.

Cover and simmer for about 30 mins. Pour into oven-proof bowl, submerge bread and scatter cheese on top. Grill or bake till brown.

Serves 1.
320 calories.

Having started the cult of the weather man on the BBC, Francis has become a celebrity in his own right. He is keenly interested in the environment as a whole, and manages to communicate his enthusiasm for country matters.

Joanna Lumley

LEEK & POTATO SOUP

2 oz (55g) butter	
4 large leeks	
4 large potatoes	
1 to 1½ pints (570 to 855ml) of hot water	
Heaped tablespoon of Marmite	
3 cloves	
Seasoning to taste	

Because fame came to her via the TV series 'The New Avengers', producers often found it difficult to see Joanna in the sort of role that she herself wanted to play. Joanna Lumley is now recognised as a fine serious actress and a particularly talented comedienne, an area to which she warms. She is a willing supporter of many animal causes.

Melt the butter in a large saucepan. Add the cleaned and chopped leeks, and the peeled and cubed potatoes. Stir them over a low heat for 3 minutes.

Pour in the water, having first dissolved the Marmite in it. Add the cloves, a little salt, and lots of black pepper. Simmer over a low heat until cooked – this should take about 30 minutes.

Check seasoning.

Serve with very soft new bread.

John Dankworth

GAZPACHO

2 ripe tomatoes, peeled and seeded
Half large cucumber, peeled and seeded
Half red or green sweet pepper, seeded
Half sweet Spanish onion
4 green onions
2 cloves garlic
Half teaspoon salt
Quarter teaspoon pepper
Half cup dry bread crumbs
3 tablespoons olive oil
2 teaspoons white vinegar
Half cup cold water
Half pound (227g) ice cubes
1 cup cold water

Finely chop the tomatoes, cucumber, pepper and onions. Place in a large bowl. Grind the garlic, salt, pepper and bread crumbs with a mortar and pestle, and add to mixture in bowl. Slowly add oil and vinegar, stirring well. Pour in the water; stir well. In a cup measure, put water and enough ice cubes to make up to cup level. Before serving, remove any bits of ice.

Decorate the gazpacho with finely chopped cucumber, onion, tomato, slices of hard boiled eggs and plain croutons. Serve with French bread.

Serves four.

This recipe is given in cups – presumably American cups as this is where John Dankworth and his wife Cleo Laine spend much of their time. You might like a translation! Half a cup of dried breadcrumbs is about 2 oz (55g) – 2 heaped tablespoons. One and a half cups of cold water is about ⅔ pint (380ml).

One of Britain's foremost saxophonists and band leaders, John Dankworth is popular throughout the world. Despite his busy schedule, he and his wife Cleo Laine find time to create special workshops for young musicians at their home near Milton Keynes.

Genial host of childrens' TV shows, and former compere of 'Game for a Laugh', Matthew is closely involved with Zoocheck. He has been a vegetarian for several years, and thrives on it.

Matthew Kelly

FRESH PEA SOUP

2 oz (55g) butter
1 lb (454g) fresh shelled peas
1 teaspoon salt
Pinch mixed herbs
1 small lettuce heart
2 pints (1.15 litres) cold water
1 teaspoon black pepper
4 teaspoons single cream

In a medium sized saucepan melt the butter until it foams. Then add the peas and the lettuce heart and gently cook for 5 mins, stirring all the time.

Then add the herbs, salt and pepper and cook for a further minute stirring frequently. Next add the water and cook for 20 mins but do not allow to boil.

When it is cooked transfer to a blender and blend until smooth. Transfer to serving bowls and add a teaspoon of cream to each portion. Serve immediately.

Tahini instead of cream makes the soup smooth and adds a slightly nutty taste.

I have from an early age abjured from the use of meat and the time will come when men such as I will look upon the murder of animals as they now look upon the murder of men.

He who does not value life does not deserve it.

LEONARDO DA VINCI

SNACKS & STARTERS

Captain Sensible

BOSTON BAKED BEANS

1 lb (455g) dried haricot beans, soaked overnight and then drained
2 onions
1 lb (455g) tomatoes
3 tablespoon molasses
2 teaspoons raw cane sugar
1-2 teaspoons mustard powder
1 teaspoon fresh mixed herbs or ½ teaspoon dried herbs
2 tablespoons tomato purée
Seasoning

Put the beans into a pan with plenty of fresh water and bring to the boil. Cover the pan and simmer the beans for 30 minutes. Drain again and reserve the water.

Chop the onions and tomatoes and put them into an ovenproof dish. Add the drained beans, molasses, sugar, mustard, herbs, tomato puree and salt and pepper to taste. Pour about ⅓ pint of the water in which the beans were cooked into the other ingredients, and stir well.

Cover the casserole and bake in a moderate oven, stirring every now and again, and adding more water if necessary. The beans will take 2-3 hours to become completely soft and absorb all the flavours. Adjust the seasoning before serving.

This is the traditional way to make baked beans. It's slow – but the beans taste great. Nothing like tinned of course!

As the beans are so slow to cook, why not make up twice the amount and keep the extra in the fridge or freezer?

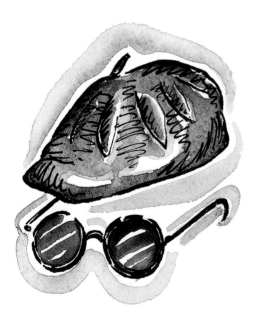

Belying his popular image as a madcap, Captain Sensible – as he was nicknamed in punk legends 'The Damned' – is serious minded about social injustice and, at the forefront of that, animal rights. He has recorded two outstanding songs on the subject, 'Torture Me' by the Damned and 'Wot! No Meat?' with his wife Rachel of the Dolly Mixtures. This song was written with Geoff Francis, a founder member of 'Enough' and was used to promote the launch of the campaign in 1985. From this title came the Wot! No Meat? sponsored vegetarian weeks which raise money for long term projects in the Third World to feed malnourished children. The Captain was the first to endorse this idea.

A wonderful nutcase, who won public acclaim in 'Not the Nine O'Clock News', Pamela Stephenson has toured internationally with her own one-woman comedy show, and has appeared on film and television as a serious actress to great acclaim. She is a musical parodist of genius.

Pamela Stephenson

CHEESE STRUDEL

This recipe was attributed to George Bernard Shaw who, as I'm sure you know, was a vegetarian. Strange that he should have been kind to animals and so beastly to women… Still, there you go!!

FOR STRUDEL:
5 oz (140g) plain flour
1 egg
1 tablespoon vegetable oil
Pinch of salt
3 tablespoons lukewarm water

FOR FILLING:
8 oz (125g) grated cheddar cheese
3 oz (85g) cooked rice
1 oz (30g) fine breadcrumbs
2 oz (55g) butter, melted
6 tablespoons cream

Sift the flour into a bowl, make a hole in the centre. Add the egg, oil, salt and water (combining them well first). Mix with a knife to make a dough then turn on to a well-floured board and knead until smooth and elastic in texture. Leave in a warm spot for 30 mins.

Place dough on a well-floured cloth and roll and stretch it until it is paper thin. Trim uneven edges.

For the filling, mix together the ingredients and season well. Spread the mixture evenly over the pastry. (If liked you can sprinkle a little finely grated onion over the mixture.) Beginning at one corner, carefully roll the pastry into a long sausage. Turn ends and pinch into place. Brush with egg and milk and cook in a moderate oven for about 40 mins. Sprinkle with poppy seeds and sugar before serving.

This recipe is from George Bernard Shaw's 'Vegetarian Cook Book' published by Pan.

Colin Spencer

AVOCADO & WATERCRESS MOUSSE

3 large ripe avocados
½ pint (285ml) smetana
1 tablespoon lime juice
1 clove garlic – crushed
Sea salt and freshly ground black pepper
1 bunch watercress
2 egg whites

Peel and stone the avocados and scrape the avocado flesh into a blender container.

Add the smetana, lime juice, garlic and seasoning and blend to a smooth purée.

Remove the watercress stalks and discard. Finely chop the leaves and add to the avocado purée. Blend again to incorporate the watercress evenly.

Pour into a bowl. Whisk the egg whites until stiff but not dry and fold into the avocado puree.

Place in the coolest part of the refrigerator and chill for 12-24 hours.

Serves 4-6

Colin Spencer is a novelist and playwright who has, in the last decade, written many vegetarian and fish cookery books, while also writing for The Guardian and New Statesman. One of his aims is to expose the corruption within the world of food distribution and food aid.

In a very short period, Bill has become one of the most popular stars of that exceptionally popular soap 'EastEnders'. His interpretation of Arthur's depression would readily grace far more demanding mediums, and has helped to set the standard which has put 'EastEnders' in a different league from any other soap.

Bill Treacher

POTATOES DAUPHINOIS À LA HAY

1 lb (455g) potatoes
3 onions
Water
¼ pint (140ml) double cream

Scrub the potatoes (leave skins on) and cut into ¼ inch slices. Chop the onions roughly. Put the vegetables into a saucepan of water and cook 8-10 mins.

Transfer the vegetables and some of the water to an overproof dish. Pour on the cream. Bake at 375°F/190°C/ Gas Mark 5 for half an hour or until browned.

Smashing with side salad. Serve hot or cold.

Christine Stone

ALMOND CARROT PANCAKES

WOT! NO MEAT?

FOR BATTER:
4 oz (115g) plain wholemeal flour
1 egg
½ pint (285ml) half milk, half water
Pinch of salt

FOR FILLING:
8 oz (225g) young carrots
1 oz (30g) raw cane sugar
1 oz (30g) butter or margarine
1 tablespoon finely grated orange peel
4 oz (115g) chopped blanched almonds
Seasoning to taste
Extra butter to top, parsley to garnish

Make the batter first by putting the flour into a bowl and stirring in the egg. Gradually add the liquid, stirring to keep it free from lumps. Flavour with salt. Whisk the batter well, then set aside in the cool for half an hour. Peel and slice the carrots (or cut them into even-sized sticks).

Stir the sugar into the melted fat, add the orange peel, nuts and seasoning, and cook gently for five mins. Add the carrots and cook gently, stirring occasionally, for about 10 mins or until the carrots are just cooked. Meanwhile make the pancakes and set them aside.

Fill each pancake with some of the carrot-and-nut mixture, fold them and arrange side by side in a heatproof dish. Top with knobs of fat, put under the grill for a few minutes, then garnish with parsley sprigs. Nice with big green salad.

Vegans can use vegan margarine. A vegan batter can be made using 4 oz (115g) plain flour, 2 oz (55g) soya flour, 1 tablespoon baking powder, ½ pint (285ml) water, plus seasoning. Whisk well, set in cool, then use in the normal way.

Pancakes made this way can of course be filled with a variety of vegetables. Some to try: mushrooms, olives, celery, sunflower seeds, spinach in cheese sauce, any left-over beans with chilli powder added, scrambled eggs, TVP sauce, stir-fried vegetables with cashew nuts.

Christine did not start modelling until her late twenties. Until then, she had been teaching English at a school in Hertfordshire where she still lives with her husband John and new daughter Alice Elizabeth. For several years she has been one of the most successful models in the popular press. Christine is second generation Animal Rights, and has been vegetarian for eighteen years. She credits her diet for the placid and delightful disposition of her daughter who was 'no puny child' but weighed eight pounds at birth. 'Alice has never suffered with spots or even nappy rash,' says Christine.

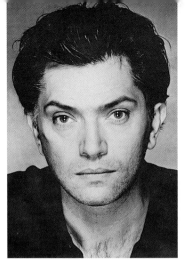

After springing to fame with the hit TV series 'The Professionals', Martin Shaw has established himself as one of the most versatile performers on the modern stage. Martin follows Sant Mat, the teachings of the Saints, and embodies the compassion that one would expect from this demanding path. He has recently also become involved in an ethical mail-order business, seeking to avoid exploiting all forms of life.

Martin Shaw

SCRAMBLED TOFU ON TOAST

Here's a quick snack recipe. As an alternative to scrambled eggs I use the more nourishing and digestible tofu. It's becoming more readily available now from health shops as well as oriental markets.

10 oz (280g) firm tofu
Approx. 3 tablespoons vegetable oil
Good pinch of turmeric
Tamari soya sauce
Good pinch cayenne
Garlic salt
Herbs to taste
4 slices thick wholemeal toast

Drain the tofu (best done by wrapping it in a clean tea-towel and leaving it with a weight on top for a short time). Use a fork to mash coarsely.

Heat the oil, add the tofu, and stir well. Add turmeric to give it colour, soya sauce to flavour. Cook briefly, stirring continually, then add the spices and herbs. Cook until heated through, which should only take 5 mins or so.

Pile the mixture on to hot wholemeal toast and eat at once.

Another good filling for pancakes?

Johnnie Walker

GUACAMOLE

1 large ripe avocado
1 large tomato, chopped
1 clove garlic, finely chopped
½ small onion, finely chopped – optional
1 tablespoon lemon juice
Good pinch cayenne pepper
Seasoning to taste

Peel and stone the avocado. Mash it to make a smooth purée. Stir all the other ingredients into the avocado and mix well. Or serve it with crisps, corn chips or tortillas. It can also be spread on bread or toast.

For variety try adding enough soured cream or plain yoghurt to give the mixture a pale creamy colour, or stir in a spoonful or two of tahini. A sprinkling of parsley sprigs on top of the dip adds colour.

One of the original pirates who joined the ranks of the BBC, fell from favour, kept his integrity and recently returned in triumph to host the 'Stereo Sequence' on Radio One. Johnny Walker is perhaps the most articulate of popular disc jockeys: during his time in commercial radio in the West Country, he never missed an opportunity to introduce questions about animal issues and vegetarianism.

Lene Lovich

SPINACH FIZZ

Her extraordinary voice was first employed in British horror movies, but she became known in her own right on the second tour organised by Stiff records, and with such hit singles as 'Lucky Number'. Lene Lovich's most recent tour was with Nina Hagen under the title 'Don't Kill the Animals', which is also the title of one of two tracks she supplied for the People For the Ethical Treatment of Animals' LP 'Animal Liberation'. In order to promote this LP, she has toured the United States and Europe extensively at her own expense.

About a half to one pound of good fresh spinach (depending on how much you like it and the size of your pan)

1 large onion – chopped

1-2 cloves of garlic – chopped (optional)

2 tablespoons oil (enough to cover the bottom of the pan)

A little lemon juice (optional)

Pepper

You'll need a large diameter frying pan, as deep as possible, with a lid.

Wash the spinach well and pick out any dodgy bits, breaking up any extra large leaves – let it drain in a colander while you do the rest.

Put oil in the pan and let it get very hot. Test by flicking a drop of water off the end of your finger; it should sizzle immediately. Add chopped onions and keep stirring so they don't burn – when they begin to go soft add the garlic and cook until they start to become transparent.

Now comes the tricky bit. Transfer the semi drained spinach to the pan and cover immediately. You will hear a big 'FIZZ' which will then go quiet. Cook one minute more and then serve with a squeeze of lemon.

Rolf Harris

BACHELOR SCRAMBLED EGGS & TOMATOES

2 eggs per person
1 tomato per person
(maybe a spring onion if you like them)
Bits of milk, butter, salt, pepper

First melt small splodge of butter (or margarine) in frypan and drop in finely cut up spring onion and cook over slow heat for short while – then add a slosh of milk – too much and eggs are watery later. Take the pan off the heat while you break eggs into pan.

Add a dusting of salt to each egg and as much pepper as you enjoy. Then, back to low heat while you graunch up the eggs with a wooden spoon and gradually scramble them around.

Must be low heat – nothing is worse than little black horrible tasting burnt bits in scrambled egg.

Meanwhile – your tomato should be cut in half and placed under grill – put flat side down first and grill until skin shrivels up and starts to go black – then turn over, add dusting of salt and grill the flat side.

Your scrambled egg should be just starting to solidify, so take it off the heat for a tick while you pop in your two beautifully grilled tomatoes.

The skin on the smooth side just comes away but you will need to cut out the core on the other half of the tomato.

Back on the heat while you squelch up the tomato with the wooden spoon. Don't dry it up too much – DELICIOUS! (Mix egg and tomato thoroughly.)

The first of the wave of Antipodean humourists to establish themselves in Britain, Rolf Harris came to Britain as an art student in 1952, and had work exhibited at the Royal Academy. He soon established himself as a light comic entertainer in 'Showcase' with Benny Hill and has since had hit singles with 'Sun Arise', 'Two Little Boys' and 'Jake the Peg'. He has performed all over the world. Rolf is an all-round talent; a songwriter, musician, sculptor and cartoonist. At the age of fifteen, he was even junior backstroke swimming champion of Australia.

John Peel

GAS HOUSE EGGS

I discovered this recipe in an old Humphrey Bogart movie!

As Beatlemania hit America, so did John Peel; by claiming intimate knowledge of the fab four, he established himself as a DJ. Since his involvement in early psychedelia he has been respected for his integrity in discerning new musical talent. He has been the means by which virtually every band of note has first come to public attention. He now broadcasts throughout the world, and is also a witty and self-deprecating writer on rock. John Peel is a long time ethical vegetarian, and it is rumoured that the only way you could get him to part with a record is to swap it for organic veg.

2 slices wholemeal bread
1 free range egg
sunflower oil or margarine

Put vegetable oil into pan, cut hole in bread with egg cup, drop egg into hole and fry in the normal way.

Serves 1

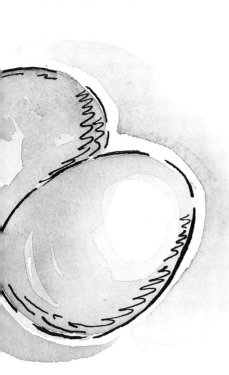

Elaine Paige

COURGETTES NIÇOISE

Preparation time 30 minutes
Cooking time 50-55 minutes

1 oz (30g) butter
6 potatoes, peeled and sliced
4 courgettes, sliced
4 onions, peeled and sliced
6 tomatoes, sliced
Salt and freshly ground black pepper
4 fl oz brandy or cognac
4 oz (115g) Gruyère cheese, grated

Melt the butter in a pan. Add the onion and cook until lightly browned. Mix with the potatoes, courgettes and tomatoes. Spoon into an ovenproof dish and season to taste with salt and pepper. Sprinkle with the brandy or cognac, cover and cook in a preheated moderately hot oven 375°F/190°C/Gas Mark 5 for 30 minutes.

Sprinkle with the cheese and cook uncovered for a further 15-20 minutes until golden. Serve very hot straight from the dish.

Serves 6

This recipe comes from a favourite book of Elaine's called 'Pocket Gourmet Vegetables' published by W.H. Smith. Series Editor: Carol Brown.

In the popular mind, Elaine Paige's name is synonymous with 'Evita', a role which she made her own on the London stage. She is a consistently successful recording star – 'I Know Him Too Well' was a duet with Barbara Dickson – and an in-demand actress.

Howard Jones

CHEESE & SWEETCORN FLAN

Howard Jones adapted the fashionable cult for synthesised music to his own warm human vocals and ecological concerns; as a result his audience ranges from new wave to new age. His songs contain reflective lyrics of personal awareness and individualist philosophy; 'Assault and Battery', a song about factory farming, was inspired by Mark Gold's book of the same title (Mark is one of the founder members of the 'Enough' project). Howard has successfully opened a vegetarian nightclub in New York.

FOR PASTRY:
7 oz (200g) 85% wholewheat flour
3½ oz (100g) margarine
Pinch salt
Few drops lemon juice

FOR FILLING:
8 oz (225g) hard cheese
1 tablespoon flour
1 small tin sweetcorn
2 free range eggs
¼ pint (150ml) single cream (or milk)

Make pastry by sifting flour and salt together: rub in the margarine, and add lemon and enough water to form a dough. Leave to rest in a cool place for an hour or so.

Lightly grease a deep flan dish and line with rolled out pastry. Grate the cheese and toss with the flour. Place half of it in the flan. Drain the sweetcorn and arrange in the dish. Cover with the remaining cheese. Beat the cream and eggs, pour the mixture over the cheese, and sprinkle with nutmeg.

Bake at 375°F/190°C/Gas Mark 5 for 40 mins.

If you're serving this as a starter – or wanted to take it on a picnic, or for a packed lunch for work – try making four small individual flans instead of one large. Cook for a shorter time, approximately 20 minutes should be long enough, but check as you go.

To my mind the life of a lamb is no less precious than that of a human being. I should be unwilling to take the life of a lamb for the sake of a human body. I hold that, the more helpless a creature, the more entitled it is to protection by man from the cruelty of man.

MOHANDAS GANDHI

PASTA

Spike Milligan

SPAGHETTI DOLCE

| Approx 8 oz (225g) spaghetti, cooked al dente, no salt (about 8 minutes) |
| 5 oz (140g) carton double cream |
| Two tablespoons brandy |
| Caster sugar to taste |

Cook spaghetti. Whilst this is cooking mix together cream, brandy and caster sugar. When spaghetti is ready pour over the cream.

There's no one who doesn't love Spike Milligan. Goon, comic genius, and under it all a sensitive and profound human being, Spike is the ready champion of things small and helpless.

Hayley Mills

SPINACH & MUSHROOM LASAGNE

As the daughter of Sir John Mills, it would have been difficult for Hayley not to have entered the theatrical profession. However, she took to it particularly early. Hayley's first appearance was in 'Tiger Bay' and the first role for which she won critical acclaim was in Bryan Forbes' highly acclaimed 'Whistle Down the Wind'. Most of her work has been in a lighter vein than this, but privately she is a serious and contemplative person, which has led her in recent years to explore 'Krishna Consciousness'.

6 oz (170g) sliced mushrooms
1 oz (30g) butter
1 vegetable stock cube
1 teaspoon soya sauce
2 lb (910g) spinach
Pinch of nutmeg
12 oz (340g) Ricotta cheese
8 pieces of cooked lasagne (follow instructions on packet)
3 oz (85g) grated Parmesan or Cheddar cheese
Seasoning to taste

Cook mushrooms gently in butter, add stock cube. Cover then add 1 teaspoon soya sauce and purée. Cook spinach gently in own juice and butter. Add nutmeg.

Add Ricotta to spinach and salt and pepper.

Lightly grease oven dish then add half cheese and spinach and cover with 4 pieces of lasagne then add half mushroom sauce then rest of spinach filling. Cover with remaining lasagne. Tuck ends in, top with rest of mushroom sauce.

Cover with grated cheese.

Cook for 35 to 40 minutes at 400°F/200°C (Gas Mark 6).

Serve with summer salad and wholewheat bread.

Paul Weller

PASTA A LA PRICEY

6 oz (170g) of various pasta shapes
1 small aubergine, cubed
1 onion, sliced
Half green pepper, sliced
Half red pepper, sliced
2 sticks of celery, chopped
6 oz (170g) cheese
1 tin of Campbell's tomato spaghetti sauce

Cook pasta until soft. Do likewise with the aubergine, onion, peppers and celery. Mix together when cooked and then add tomato sauce (I've checked the ingredients of this sauce and it's OK for vegetarians.)

Serve when mixture is hot, that's it!!

Serves 2

Aubergine can be rather bitter. To remove the juices that cause this, cut it into thick slices, arrange on a plate, sprinkle with salt and set aside for about half an hour. Then rinse the aubergine in cold water and pat dry with a clean teatowel or cloth. Cut into cubes. It's now ready to use in the above – or any other! – recipe.

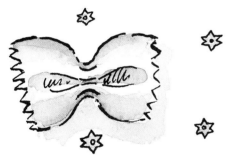

Tim Barker

PASTA & BEANS

Travelled gourmets may know that in Naples they specialise in a thick beany soup/stew called 'Pasta e Fagioli'. This does not claim to be it!

Unless you are a reader of 'Punch', for whom he has compiled the Christmas crossword for the past two years, it might be that you will not recognise the name of Tim Barker. However, it is unlikely that his face is unknown to you. He appears regularly in adverts with the likes of Arthur Daley and in cameo performances in a number of English films. He has also appeared in 'Brookside'.

Cooking oil
Half an onion, chopped very finely
2 cloves of garlic, crushed
1 tomato, finely chopped
Tomato puree
Salt and black pepper
4 oz (115g) small pasta shells or other pasta bits
¾ lb (340g) or a 14 oz (395g) tin of white kidney (canellini) beans

Prepare the beans beforehand if you want to use fresh ingredients. As a child of the twentieth century I just open a tin.

In a large, stout saucepan – one of those cast iron enamel things is even better – begin to saute the onion and garlic. Chop the tomato and stir it in along with the puree. Add *liberal* amounts of salt and particularly pepper and simmer for 5 minutes.

Add 1 pint (570ml) of water and bring to the boil, stirring advisedly. Add the pasta, bring back to the boil and cook until the pasta is 'al dente' – or 'ready' as we say in English.

Drain the beans and tip them in. Continue to heat for 5 minutes or so. Eat.

Feeds two.

If this basic recipe seems over-bland, then next time add a seasoning or herbs of your choice.

Martin Shaw

PASTA WITH TVP SAUCE

When using TVP, cook in with other ingredients. It will have a much better flavour. Use the mixture in pies too.

5 oz (140g) TVP mince, hydrated in water
2 tablespoons vegetable oil
1 large onion
1-2 cloves of garlic, crushed
Herbs to taste
Seasoning to taste
Tamari soya sauce

Drain TVP. Heat the oil and fry the sliced onion for a few minutes to soften. Add the garlic, stir and fry a few minutes more. Add TVP, herbs, seasoning, a generous amount of tamari soya sauce and a little of the water in which the TVP was soaked.

Allow the sauce to simmer until the water has evaporated and it will be ready to serve.

This sauce is very good with pasta. Cook approximately 8 oz (225g) wholemeal spaghetti or tagliatelle whilst the sauce is simmering.

A woman of strong commitment to social and Third World issues. As an actress her range of skills is legendary; she can play comedy or the most demanding of dramatic roles, on stage or on film.

Glenda Jackson

RED HOT MARROW

1 oz butter
1 small onion, thinly sliced
1 clove of garlic, chopped finely
1 heaped teaspoon paprika and ¼ teaspoon of cayenne pepper
1 small marrow, peeled and cut into one-inch pieces
8 oz (225g) firm tomatoes, skinned and sliced

Melt the butter in a saucepan over a low heat, then stir in onion, garlic, paprika and cayenne and cover. Simmer for ten minutes then stir in cubes of marrow.

Season, cover again and cook for a further ten minutes. Add tomatoes, cover again and cook for another five minutes.

This vegetable dish is especially good with pasta. Cook 10 oz (285g) pasta shells – the mixed green and white look attractive. Drain the shells, top with Red Hot Marrow, lots of fresh parsley and a sprinkling of sunflower seeds or grated cheese.

Lentil & Red Pepper Sauce

Howard Jones

LENTIL & RED PEPPER SAUCE

1 onion, peeled and chopped
1 small red pepper, de-seeded and chopped
2 tablespoons oil
1 clove garlic, crushed
1 teaspoon basil
10 oz (255g) can tomatoes
4 oz (115g) split red lentils
1 tablespoon tomato purée
¾ pint (425ml) salted water
½ oz (15g) butter
Salt and pepper
A pinch of sugar
12 oz (340g) wholewheat spaghetti
Grated cheese to serve

Fry the onion and pepper in oil in a large saucepan for 10 minutes, then put in garlic, basil, tomatoes, lentils, tomato purée and salted water. Bring to the boil, then turn down the heat to simmer gently uncovered for 15-20 minutes until the lentils are cooked. Season with salt and pepper and a dash of sugar.

About 15 minutes before the sauce is ready, half fill a large saucepan with lightly salted water and bring to the boil.

Add the pasta, easing the pasta down into the water as the ends soften. Boil rapidly, uncovered, for about 10 minutes, until a piece feels tender when you bite it. Drain, then return to the pan with the butter, salt and pepper.

Serve with the sauce and hand around the grated cheese.

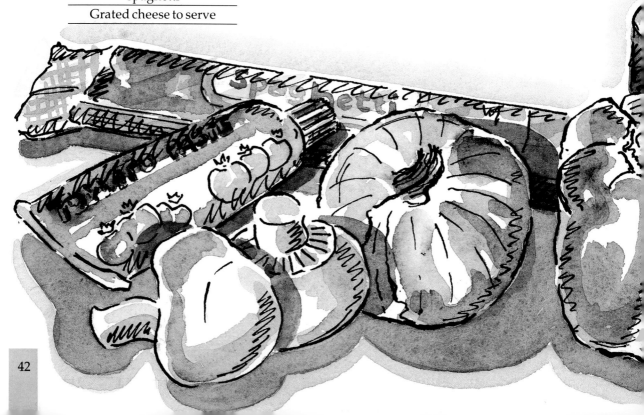

Maureen Duffy has published plays, poetry and non-fiction – including her startling survey 'The Erotic World of Faerie' – but is best known as a novelist. She wrote the first novel to take animal liberation as its theme, 'I Want to Go to Moscow', and has also produced a handbook on animal rights, 'Men and Beasts', as well as a recent collection of poetry based on nature and animals.

Maureen Duffy

SPAGHETTI NAPOLI

2 tablespoons vegetable oil
1 medium sized onion
2 cloves garlic, crushed
4 oz (115g) mushroom
1 medium tin Italian plum tomatoes
Seasoning to taste
Italian tomato paste
Fresh herbs
Half glass dry red wine
8-10 oz (225-280g) spaghetti
2 oz (55g) butter
Parmesan cheese

Heat the oil. Slice and fry the onion until soft, together with the garlic cloves. Slice and add the mushrooms. Add the tomatoes, seasoning and several squirts or a small tin of tomato paste. If available, flavour with fresh herbs – parsley, basil, rosemary and a bay leaf. Stir well and leave to simmer with all the ingredients combined to make a sauce. At the last moment add the wine.

Meanwhile, cook the spaghetti in a large pan of boiling water. Serve the sauce over the well-drained pasta, add knobs of butter and grated Parmesan cheese.

You can adapt this basic sauce by stirring in one of the following: cooked lentils, left over hummous, a few spoonfuls of plain yoghurt, cooked TVP mince, tahini etc.

Tagliatelle with Mushroom Sauce

Matthew Kelly

TAGLIATELLE WITH MUSHROOM SAUCE

2 oz butter
2 cloves fresh garlic chopped
1 onion finely chopped
1 teaspoon salt and pepper
1 teaspoon mixed herbs
1 lb (455g) fresh mushrooms chopped
1 pint water
2 teaspoons cornflour mixed with 2 teaspoons cold water
3 tablespoons single cream
10 oz (280g) white or wholemeal tagliatelle

First melt the butter, then add the chopped garlic, onion, salt, pepper, and herbs. Gently fry in a saucepan until you can see through the onion – beware of over-cooking.

Next add the mushrooms and gently fry for 2 minutes (these will absorb all the surplus butter). Gently pour in the water and bring to the boil, turn heat down immediately and simmer for 10 minutes.

Add the cornflour mixture and bring back to the boil – your sauce should thicken at this stage. At the last minute add the cream and wait 10 seconds for it to heat through. Serve at once with the tagliatelle.

Most people prefer their own particular brand of pasta so I have left it to your taste. Simply follow the instructions on the box, bearing in mind that this dish is a very quick one and needs to be served as soon as the cream is heated through to get the best results.

Clare Francis

VEGETARIAN LASAGNE

It is hard to conceive the strength of will and pure determination that it takes to sail solo across the Atlantic, but this is what Clare Francis achieved, the first woman so to do. She has gone on to become a best-selling author, and has shown a similar sense of purpose in campaigning on behalf of animals. Recently she has launched a campaign against the use of animals for fur, and is closely associated with the organisation Lynx.

1 large onion, sliced
1½ green peppers, sliced
8 oz (225g) mushrooms, sliced
1 lb (445g) aubergines, cubed
Grated carrots (optional)
8 oz (225g) courgettes, sliced (optional)
8 oz (225g) lasagne
1 tin tomatoes
Tomato purée
½ pint (285ml) vegetable stock
1 tin kidney beans
Salt and pepper
Herbs
Fresh basil if available
½ pint (285ml) bechamel sauce
Grated Cheddar or Mozzarella cheese

Gently cook onions, peppers and mushrooms for about 10 minutes, plus carrots if you wish. Meanwhile, steam aubergines and courgettes for about 10 minutes. Add tomato purée to fried vegetables and mix well.

Add the tinned kidney beans, tomatoes and the freshly steamed vegetables. Stir gently and simmer for 5-10 minutes.

Take freshly cooked pasta (or pre-cooked variety) and starting with the tomato sauce alternate with layers of pasta finishing with layer of sauce.

Top the dish with bechamel sauce and grated Cheddar cheese or Mozzarella.

Bake at 400°F/200°C (Gas Mark 6) for 20-25 minutes.

The fate of animals is of greater importance to me than the fear of appearing ridiculous; it is indissolubly connected with the fate of men.

EMILE ZOLA

SALADS

Bryan Forbes

MINTED WHEAT SALAD

8 oz (225g) bulghar wheat
Bunch of spring onions
Handful of raisins
2 oz (55g) pumpkin seeds, roasted
Few sprigs of mint, chopped
Grated rind and juice of 1 small lemon
1 clove garlic, crushed
6 tablespoons olive oil or sunflower oil
Salt and pepper
Lettuce hearts to serve (optional)

Soak the bulghar in cold water for about 30 minutes, then drain it thoroughly and put the grains in a bowl. Chop the spring onions and add them to the bulgar with the raisins, pumpkin seeds and mint.

In a screw-topped jar mix the lemon rind and juice, garlic, oil and plenty of seasoning. Shake well, then pour this dressing over the salad and toss. Marinate for at least 30 minutes. Arrange on lettuce leaves.

Other nuts go well with this recipe, particularly chopped walnuts. If there is any left over, mix it with a little lightly beaten egg, shape into a patty, and fry on both sides.

Bryan Forbes was a prodigy. In his teens, he was chairman of a 'Junior Brains Trust' radio quiz. By his early twenties he had published the first of his many books and gained his first screen credit as a writer in 'Cockleshell Heroes'. Forbes' biography of Edith Evans was definitive, and he is a fine actor. However, his main achievement is as a film director who takes on difficult subjects, sensitively dealt with. 'Whistle Down the Wind', 'The L-Shaped Room', 'The Whisperers' – with Edith Evans – and 'The Raging Moon' are among his best films. He is a master of understatement and draws strong performances from his stars.

BEETROOT SALAD

1 Iceberg lettuce
1 lb (445g) beetroot
Grated rind and juice of a lemon
Celery salt and pepper
6 tablespoons olive oil
Pinch of salt
¼ pint (140ml) soured cream
Bunch of chives chopped
½ oz (12g) sugar

Put the sliced lettuce on a serving dish. Peel and grate the beetroot, put in a bowl and toss in the lemon rind and juice, celery salt and pepper to taste, oil and sugar. Pile the beetroot on top of the lettuce, pour the soured cream over the top with the chives.

SCRUBBED POTATO SALAD

2 lb (910g) small new potatoes
1 bunch spring onions
½ lb (225g) shelled peas, cooked
Small bunch of fresh basil or marjoram, chopped
½ pint (140ml) olive oil
1 fl oz (24ml) cider vinegar
½ clove garlic, crushed
1 teaspoons caster sugar
½ tablespoon mild wholegrain mustard

Scrub the potatoes and cook them in boiling salted water until tender – about 10 minutes. Drain thoroughly.

Chop the onions and sprinkle them over the hot potatoes, adding the peas and herbs. Put the remaining ingredients in a liquidiser or food processor and whizz them up until thoroughly combined. Pour this dressing over and toss the potatoes in it to coat them all completely. Cool, then chill the salad.

This (together with the other recipes contributed by Nanette Newman) is taken from her 'Summer Cookbook', published by Hamlyn, copyright Bryan Forbes Ltd., 1986, and reproduced with many thanks.

Salad in a Boat

Virginia McKenna

SALAD IN A BOAT

Approx 1 pint (570ml) water
2 oz (55g) butter or margarine
1-4 teaspoons salt
8-12 oz (225-340g) plain flour
3 eggs
3 oz (85g) shredded Swiss cheese
½ lb (225g) small spinach leaves
Egg and Vegetable Salad (as under)
8 cherry tomatoes

In a 2 quart pan bring water, butter and salt to the boil. When butter melts, remove pan from heat and add flour at once. Beat until well blended.

Return to medium heat and stir rapidly for one minute or until a ball forms in the middle of the pan and a film forms on the bottom of the pan.

Remove pan from heat and beat in eggs, one at a time, until mixture is smooth and glossy. Add cheese and beat until well mixed. Spoon into a greased 9-inch round pan with removable bottom or spring-release sides.

Bake crust in oven 200°C/ 400°F (Gas Mark 6) for 40 minutes or until puffed and brown; turn off oven. With a wooden pick, prick crust in 10 or 12 places; leave in closed oven for about 10 minutes to dry. Remove pan from oven and cool completely. Remove crust from pan: this is the 'boat'.

Prepare egg and vegetable salad. Line bottom and sides of boat with spinach leaves. Cut each tomato in half. Pile egg salad over spinach and garnish with cherry tomatoes. Cut in thick wedges.

Makes 6 servings.

EGG AND VEGETABLE SALAD

In a bowl, stir together ½ cup mayonnaise, 1 teaspoon dijon mustard and ¼ teaspoon ground cumin. Stir in 1 cup thinly sliced raw cauliflower, ¼ pound raw mushrooms (thinly sliced), 1 cup frozen peas (thawed), 1 cup thinly sliced celery, and 2 green onions and tops (thinly sliced). Coarsely chop 6 hard-boiled free-range eggs; gently fold into vegetable mixture.

Virginia and her husband Bill Travers became almost synonymous with concern for African wildlife through a series of films like 'Born Free', 'Living Free', and 'An Elephant called Slowly'. They have put this connection to good use by starting the very necessary and effective charity Zoocheck. They work actively to close down what are often simply concentration camps for animals; zoos and circuses. Instead, they attempt to get people to appreciate animals in their natural environment.

Carla Lane

COTTAGE CHEESE SALAD

I look upon the kitchen as a tiled cell, therefore everything I make is quick and easy.

2 large bananas	
1 large avocado	
1 large green apple	
8 oz (225g) cottage cheese	
Iceberg or other lettuce and watercress for base	

Known as 'the gentle script writer', Carla Lane is the author of those much-loved series 'The Liver Birds', 'Solo', 'Butterflies', and most recently the ratings-topping 'Bread'. She introduces her concern for animals wherever she can, and has a menagerie of cast-off pets at her home in Holland Park. Carla has been vegetarian for twenty-two years, and has recently been changing to a vegan diet. Her greatest ambition is to set up a trust for animals, a dream which is about to come true. Carla is a co-founder of Animaline.

Slice the bananas into thick chunks. Peel the avocado, remove the stone, cut the fruit into thick wedges. Slice the apple.

Pile the cottage cheese on a base of coarsely shredded lettuce. Arrange watercress sprigs around the edge. Pile the prepared fruit on top. Eat at once.

The banana, avocado and apple will keep their colour if you squeeze a drop of lemon juice on them first. Any fruit is nice in this kind of salad. Nuts sprinkled on top go well too.

We love animals, we watch them with delight, we study their habits with ever-increasing curiosity; and we destroy them. The overwhelming majority eat their kinsmen without a thought.

LORD (KENNETH) CLARK

MAIN MEALS

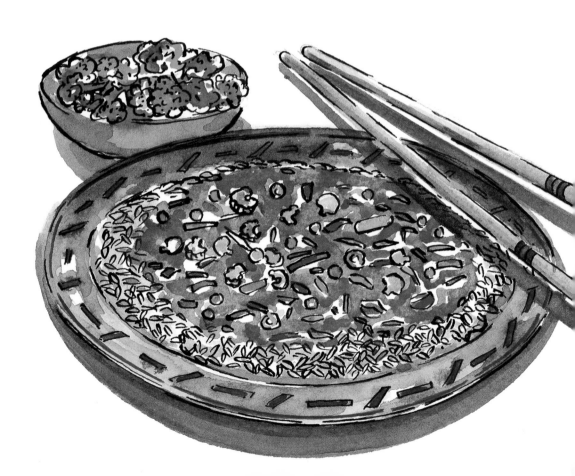

John Dankworth and Cleo Laine

CHEESE & WALNUT ROAST

8 oz (225g) walnuts
6 oz (170g) fresh brown breadcrumbs
3 oz (85g) Cheddar cheese, finely grated
1 medium onion, finely grated
2 level teaspoons salt
2 level teaspoons finely chopped parsley
Mixed herbs to taste
5 tablespoons hot milk
1 level teaspoon prepared mustard
1 level tablespoon tomato paste
Pepper to taste
½ oz (15g) polyunsaturated margarine

Preheat oven to moderate 350°F/180°C/Gas Mark 4. Line baking tray with foil and grease lightly.

Grind nuts and mix thoroughly with all ingredients except margarine. Shape into loaf approx. 3 inches high and stand it on prepared tray. Dot with flakes of margarine and bake in centre of oven for 45 mins.

Serve sliced.

Serves 4.

A lady with a very special voice first utilised in the jazz medium. In the last few years she has become a superb interpreter of standards and straight songs, which has also brought her chart success.

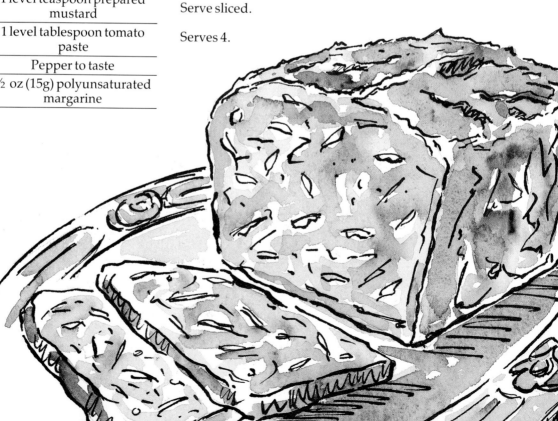

Wendy Craig

CREAMY VEGETABLE CRUMBLE

Star of Carla Lane's 'Butterflies' and an actress who has made her mark in light comedy. Her own favourite role was that of Middie Paradock in 'A Resounding Tinkle', but she has also starred in plays ranging from Ibsen's 'A Doll's House' to 'Peter Pan'. Wendy Craig has appeared in many films, including 'The Servant' and 'The Nanny', and the popular television series 'Not in Front of the Children', for which the Variety Club named her BBC TV Personality of the Year.

4 oz (115g) onion peeled and chopped
2 tablespoons vegetable oil
1 packet celery soup mix
¼ pint (140ml) evaporated milk
16 oz (455g) tin baked beans
16 oz (455g) tin carrots
3 oz (85g) margarine
6 oz (170g) plain flour

Fry the onion in the oil over a low heat for about 6 mins. Meanwhile make up half the packet of soup mix adding the evaporated milk to the soup. Place beans, carrots, onions and soup in a 2 pint pie dish.

Make the crumble by rubbing the margarine into the flour. Add the rest of the soup mix to this and sprinkle it on top of the vegetables. Bake in a moderate oven for 40 mins.

You can add grated cheese to the crumble mix if you desire.

This sort of crumble topping can be used on any vegetable base. Add chopped nuts and/or herbs for variety.

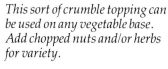

Peter Gabriel

NUTMEAT GUNGE LOAF

GUNGE:
2½ tablespoons butter
1 chopped onion
2 small cloves garlic, minced
¼ teaspoon ground cumin
¼ teaspoon thyme
¼ teaspoon marjoram
¼ teaspoon paprika
2 tablespoons flour
¾ cup vegetable broth
½ cup red wine
1½ cups broken, shelled chestnuts
2½ cups broken, shelled walnuts
½ cup broken, shelled pecans
1 cup diced celery
1 tablespoon Worcester sauce
1 tablespoon cognac
2 eggs, lightly beaten
2 tablespoons chopped fresh parsley
1 teaspoon salt
Fresh-ground black pepper to taste
½ cup dry breadcrumbs (more if needed)
4 oz grated Gruyère cheese

LOAF:
3 packets dried yeast
½ teaspoon sugar
¾ cup lukewarm milk
4 cups flour, more as needed
2 teaspoons salt
10 large egg yolks
½ cup butter, well softened

Peter Gabriel came to prominence as lead singer with the rock group Genesis, with whom he became noted for his own bizarre brand of showmanship. He has since used his solo career to pursue a more serious range of subject matter, from his anthem 'Biko' to his instigation of the WOMAD festivals, which bring together musicians from all over the world. Gabriel continues to combine state of the art studio technology with a sense of compassion and the heartbeat of African rhythms.

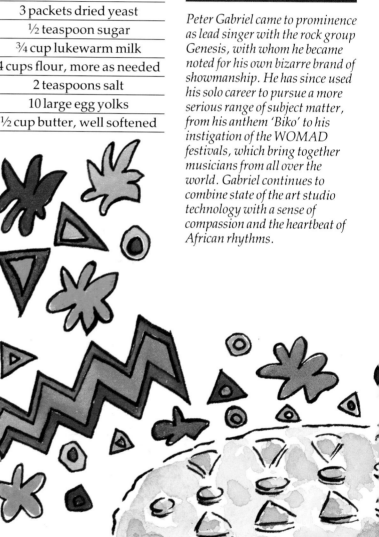

Gunge: Melt the butter in a medium-size, heavy-bottomed skillet and sauté the onion and garlic in it. When the onion turns transparent, stir in the cumin, thyme, marjoram, paprika, and flour. Allow the roux to cook for a few minutes, then add the vegetable broth and the wine, stirring with a whisk. When the sauce thickens, remove it from the heat and set aside.

Put the nutmeat and the celery through the medium blade of food mill. Stir in the sauce and all the remaining ingredients. Taste and correct seasoning.

Loaf: Prepare the dough.

Butter a loaf pan and preheat the oven to 400°. Sprinkle the yeast and sugar on the milk and let it stand for about 10 mins. Put 3 cups of the flour in a large bowl with the salt, egg yolks, and the well-softened butter. Add the yeast mixture and mix well to make a soft dough. Turn out onto a lightly floured board and knead in 1 more cup of flour. Knead for 10 to 15 minutes, until the dough no longer sticks to your hands.

Transfer the dough to a lightly buttered bowl and flip it over so that all sides are greased. Cover the bowl with a tea towel and leave the dough in a warm place to rise for 1½ to 2 hours. Punch it

down, knead for 2 or 3 minutes, and let it rise again until it is doubled in size. Punch down once more and roll it out into a rectangle about 12 inches by 15 inches.

Pile the gunge mixture carefully in an oblong shape down the centre of the dough rectangle, leaving several inches at each end and enough room on the long sides for them to overlap by about an inch over the top. Brush the edges with a little water, and seal the overlapping edges firmly. Trim the ends, tuck them up as if wrapping a package, and seal. Pinch the seams securely. Place the loaf in the pan, seam side down, and brush the top with a little beaten egg yolk. Decorate the loaf with pastry cut-outs made from the trimmings and brush the decoration with egg yolk. Bake for 20 mins at 400°F/200°C/Gas Mark 6, then for 40 mins more at 350°F/180°C/Gas Mark 4.

Variation: Peel and core 2 or 3 small green apples and fit them inside the gunge as you arrange it on the dough. The centres of the apples should be filled with gunge and they should be covered with it on all sides. Proceed as above.

Serve hot or chilled.

Makes 10 to 12 servings.

Two Bean Winter Stew with Mustard Dumplings

Janice Long

TWO-BEAN WINTER STEW WITH MUSTARD DUMPLINGS

FOR STEW:
1 large onion
Vegetable margarine
1 cup fresh mushrooms
1 medium diced potato
1 cup diced swede or turnip
3 cups cooked soybeans
1 can (small) red kidney beans
1 medium leek

AND TO TASTE:
Molasses
Soy sauce
Dijon mustard
Vegetable bouillon
Bay leaves

FOR DUMPLINGS:
4 oz (115g) self raising flour
2 oz (55g) vegetable suet, shredded
1 teaspoon dry mustard
2 tablespoons milk

Sauté onion in margarine until soft. Add mushrooms (sliced), and diced potato and turnip. Add soybeans (together with some of their cooking liquid) and rest of ingredients. Season to taste. Cook until ingredients are done, then transfer to casserole, add dumplings and bake at 350°F/180°C/Gas Mark 4 for approximately 40 mins.

For the dumplings, sieve the flour into a bowl. Add mustard and mix. Add shredded suet and mix to a dough with milk. Knead lightly on a floured board. Roll into balls. Add to stew.

Makes 8 or 9 balls.

A rare phenomenon in what often appears to be a bastion of male chauvinism, Janice appeared as a record presenter on BBC Radio One. Her programme has introduced a degree of social concern which is not readily recognised as being the realm of popular radio. She was one of the presenters in the Aids Information Service. Janice left the BBC to have a baby and has joined 'Radio, Radio'.

The face and the shape of the sixties, Twiggy successfully made the transition to other fields. Her starring role in Ken Russell's 'The Boyfriend' was touchingly vulnerable and a tour-de-force; she has since become a well known face on television. Twiggy's singing career began in the mid-seventies with her hit version of Country Joe's song 'Here I go again'. Recently, she has pursued a career in films.

Twiggy

LENTIL & MUSHROOM AU GRATIN

2 tablespoons oil
1 onion chopped
2 carrots chopped
2 celery sticks, chopped
1 clove garlic, crushed
8 oz (225g) red lentils
1 pint (570ml) water
2 tablespoons soya sauce
Salt and pepper

MUSHROOM FILLING:

1 oz (30g) margarine
8 oz (225g) flat mushrooms, sliced
2 cloves garlic, crushed
3 tablespoons chopped parsley

TO FINISH:

3 oz (85g) Cheddar cheese, grated

Heat oil in a pan, add the onion, carrot and celery and fry gently for 10 mins, until softened. Add remaining ingredients, with salt and pepper to taste. Cover and simmer for 50 mins to 1 hour, stirring occasionally until lentils are tender.

Meanwhile prepare filling. Melt margarine in frying pan, add mushrooms and fry for 2 mins, stirring. Add garlic, parsley, salt and pepper to taste, and mix well.

Place half the lentil mixture in an oiled shallow ovenproof dish. Spread the mushrooms over the top, then cover with the remaining lentil mixture. Top with the cheese and bake in preheated moderately hot oven 375°F/190°C/Gas Mark 5 for 20-25 minutes until golden and bubbling.

Robert Wyatt

CHEESE & LENTIL PIE

8 oz (225g) red lentils
1 large-ish onion (chopped small)
Oil for frying onion
6 oz (170g) grated cheese
3 oz (85g) broken cashew nuts
Large segment garlic
Salt and pepper
Half teaspoon herbs (marjoram, thyme, or mixed)
2 tablespoons breadcrumbs
2 tablespoons sesame seeds
A pinch of mace

OPTIONAL EXTRAS:

One chopped green pepper
Half green chilli
Sliced tomatoes on top

Boil lentils for 2 minutes. Drain. Fry onions till half cooked. Mix lentils, onions, 3 oz cheese, cashew, salt and pepper, herbs and chopped garlic.

Press mixture into greased flat pottery dish (so it's no more than 2 in. deep) and cover with grated cheese. Sprinkle with breadcrumbs, sesame seeds and mace. Cover with foil; bake at 400°F/200°C/Gas Mark 6 for 45 mins. Remove foil; bake further 15 mins till crisp on top.

First gaining prominence as drummer in the late sixties with the 'Soft Machine', a unique fusion of avant-garde jazz with rock music, and despite a tragic accident, Robert Wyatt has managed to stay in the forefront of contemporary music. He remains hugely influential, a musician's musician and a lovely man.

Anneka displays all the energy one would expect of someone on a healthy diet. She is the frenetic adventurer in Channel 4's extremely popular 'Treasure Hunt' and is the envy of most armchair travellers as she circumnavigates the earth for one travel show or another.

Anneka Rice

ALMOND & MUSHROOM BAKE

6 oz (170g) ground almonds
6 oz (170g) wholemeal breadcrumbs
6 oz (170g) button mushrooms
6 oz (170g) carrots
1 onion
1 clove garlic
1 stick celery
Teaspoonful olive oil
2 tablespoonsful fresh chopped parsley
¾ teaspoonful dried thyme
Freshly ground black pepper
2 free range eggs
2 tablespoonsful vegetable stock

Place the ground almonds in a large mixing bowl and stir in the breadcrumbs. Wipe the mushrooms and chop finely. Scrub the carrots and grate finely.

Mix the mushrooms and carrots into the breadcrumb mixture. Finely chop the onions, garlic and celery and cook over a low heat in the oil for 3 mins without browning.

Add to the contents of the bowl with the parsley, thyme and pepper. Beat the eggs and pour onto the mixture with the stock. Mix in thoroughly to bind the mixture.

Oil a 2 lb loaf tin and place the mixture inside, pressing down firmly. Cover with foil and place in the centre of a pre-heated oven at 375°F/190°C/Gas Mark 5 for 25 mins.

Remove foil and cook for a further 10 mins uncovered.

Serve either hot or cold.

Serves 4.

Sylvia Marriott

FESTIVE PIE

7 tablespoons 100% S.R. wholemeal flour	
1 tablespoon Soyolk	
½ teaspoon baking powder	
4 oz (115g) vegetable margarine	
Little cold water to mix	

FOR FILLING:
Tube of Italian tomato purée
Sprinkle of Froment
1 large Spanish onion
2 medium courgettes
1 red or green pepper
1 crushed garlic
Either 4 oz (115g) mushrooms or 1 tin whole chestnuts
4 oz (115g) Mozzarella cheese
Mild paprika

Rub margarine into flour and Soyolk, add baking powder when crumbled together. Put 2 level tablespoons of dry crumble aside, then add a little cold water to pastry mix. Sprinkle flour in a flan case or a sandwich tin, and press pastry into tin.

Prepare the filling:

Simmer finely cut vegetables in a tablespoon of oil or a tablespoon of water till tender. Add crushed garlic, seasoning, mushrooms or chestnuts. Put vegetable mixture into pastry case. Sprinkle Froment over pie shell to soak up all excess moisture. (If, however, the vegetable mix is too dry, add a little yoghurt, sour cream, or beaten eggs.)

Squeeze tomato purée from tube, then sprinkle reserved crumbled pastry over the filling. Top with thinly sliced Mozzarella cheese. Sprinkle with mild paprika. Bake at 400°F/200°C/Gas Mark 6 for about 40 mins on the middle shelf.

Serve with homemade rose-hip jelly or crab apple and lemon jelly.

Sylvia is famous as the archetypal sophisticated sprightly pensioner in so many TV and poster adverts. She is a delightful and tireless worker on behalf of animals and humans and is the founder of the Strawberry Vegetarian Homes for Children.

Recognised as a classical violinist without equal ever since his first public appearance in San Francisco at the age of seven, Yehudi Menuhin has explored other musical forms, including jazz and classical Indian; his interest in things Eastern extends into his daily life. He is noted for his encouragement of young musicians, and founded a school for them at Stoke D'Abernon in Surrey.

Yehudi Menuhin

STUFFED AUBERGINES

4 large aubergines
2 onions, finely chopped
2 cloves crushed garlic
4-6 ozs (115-170g) thinly sliced fresh mushrooms
4 large ripe red tomatoes, skinned, seeded and chopped
1 tablespoon tomato purée
Some stoned black olives
3 oz (85g) brown breadcrumbs
3 oz (85g) grated Gruyère cheese
½ pint (285ml) stock
2 tablespoons chopped parsley
Marjoram, thyme, oregano

Cut the aubergines in half lengthwise; scoop out the pulp, leaving the shells intact. Salt and drain the shells for about 30 mins, then rinse and dry carefully.

Fry the onions, aubergine pulp, and mushrooms gently in some butter till very soft. Add the tomatoes, purée, herbs, garlic and stock, stirring well, and finally the olives.

Mix the breadcrumbs, cheese and parsley, and add the cooked tomato mixture to them. Paint the skin of each halved aubergine with olive oil, and pile the mixture into each half. Bake in a covered dish in a moderate oven until the shells have softened and are cooked through.

Nuts go well with this recipe – especially pine nuts.

Tim Wheater

VEGETABLE CURRY

6 tablespoons good oil
Some mustard seeds (according to taste)
2/2½ inch ginger root – chopped finely
2 cloves garlic
1 large finely chopped onion
1 finely chopped green chilli
2 tablespoons turmeric
1 tablespoon ground coriander
1 teaspoon curry powder (according to taste)
8 oz (225g) fresh puréed coconut, or the equivalent creamed coconut
½ pint (285ml) vegetable stock
1½-2 lb (680g-910g) fresh vegetables in season

SIDE DISHES

Any of the following:
1 cucumber, and yoghurt to taste
Raisins soaked in water
Chopped pineapple
Roasted cashew nuts
Burnt onion in sour cream
Dahl
Chutneys
Bananas
Grated carrot soaked in lemon juice/orange juice
Salt and pepper to taste.

Heat oil over medium heat, add mustard seeds, ginger and garlic and fry quickly for a minute or less. Over reduced heat add onion and chilli and gently fry until onion is transparent or golden.

Add turmeric, coriander and curry powder and stir in well. Add vegetables and mix really thoroughly to coat them properly. Add coconut purée and vegetable stock. Stir well. Add more water if the ingredients are too dry.

Cover and simmer for 20-30 mins or until the vegetables are cooked to your own taste. (The crisper the better.)

Serve with brown rice.

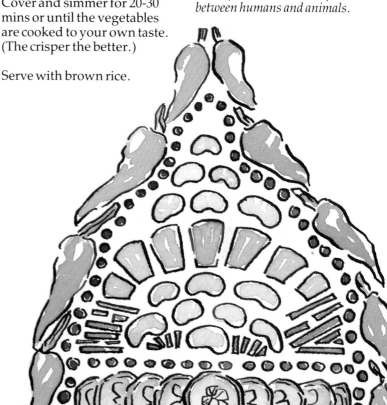

Tim found fame with The Eurythmics, before returning to his classical roots and becoming one of the most accomplished exponents of new age music. He was chosen by the World Wildlife Fund to be the British representative at the Jubilee celebrations in Assisi, where he performed alongside – amongst other – Buddhist monks and African singers in an event which sought to establish a new and more spiritual relationship between humans and animals.

A child star in the British children's cinema, Michael has all the attributes of an old fashioned troubadour. His indefatigable energy has brought him success on TV as Frank Spencer, on the stage in 'Barnum' and 'The Phantom of the Opera', in film and on record.

Michael Crawford

POTATO & CHEESE CASSEROLE

½ pint (285ml) white sauce
1 lb (454g) potatoes
8 oz (225g) Cheddar cheese
2 onions, peeled and sliced

Make a white sauce. Cut thin layers of potato and slices of cheese and onions. In an ovenproof dish, alternate layers of potato and cheese with onion and white sauce until all the ingredients have been used up. Grate cheese on top and place in hot oven at 375°F/190°C/Gas Mark 5.

For a quick meal, serve with a green salad. As a starter, coddle in individual ramekins.

Maureen Duffy

MOZZARELLA ESCALOPES

10 oz (280g) Mozzarella cheese
1 large egg yolk
seasoning
2-4 oz (55-115g) dry breadcrumbs
Vegetable oil
1 lemon
Coarse seed mustard to serve – optional

Cut the Mozzarella into slices about half an inch thick. Whisk the egg yolk lightly and season.

Dip the cheese into the egg yolk and then the breadcrumbs. Fry quickly in hot oil, turning once. Drain off any excess oil. Serve the escalopes with slices of lemon and coarse seed mustard.

A really quick way to make cheese into your protein dish – good with tiny new potatoes and a salad on hot summer days.

After coming to prominence as the protagonist of the film 'Breaking Glass', Hazel O'Connor has established herself as a fine actress. A follower of Krishna, Hazel's beliefs have helped her tread a thoughtful path through the vagaries of the rock business. She has more recently starred in a West End musical.

Hazel O'Connor

NUTTY SHEPHERD'S PIE

3 lb (1.4kg) potatoes
8 oz (225g) TVP hydrate in water
3 oz (85g) mixed chopped nuts, roasted
1 oz (30g) butter
1 clove garlic, crushed
½ teaspoon chopped chillies
2 carrots, sliced
½ small cabbage, sliced
2 sticks celery, sliced
Soya sauce
2 teaspoons Vecon
Parsley to garnish
Grated cheese

Boil the potatoes until soft. Mash them well, adding cream and/or butter if you like, and set aside. Drain TVP, add the nuts.

Melt the butter and sauté the garlic for a few minutes. Add the chillies and mix in the TVP. Cook the carrots, cabbage and celery in water to soften. Add soya sauce, Vecon, the TVP with nuts.

Pile the mixture into an ovenproof dish, top with the potatoes and smooth the surface.

Bake at 350°F/180°C/Gas Mark 4 for 20 mins. Sprinkle with cheese and cook 5-10 mins more.

Serve with chopped parsley to garnish.

Peter Cox

TEMPEH MARINADE

I can't claim any original input into this recipe, because it was developed by my wife Peggy. It is very simple to make and although it needs to be left for 6-8 hours to marinate, you'll find the preparation time well justified by the stunning taste. Served with a selection of lightly steamed fresh vegetables (especially broccoli) it makes a tremendous centrepiece to a dinner, especially if you want to knock a few meat-eaters' prejudices. Tempeh is, of course, made from fermented soya beans and is high in protein, calcium, phosphorus, iron and the vitamin B group (including B12). The more I learn about the bountiful soya bean, the more respect I have for it.

Peter Cox was born on 31st May 1955 and spent the first two years of his life in the shadow of the Sellafield reactor, Britain's dirtiest nuclear installation. Living in Norfolk then in London, he worked in advertising, then became the first Chief Executive of the Vegetarian Society of the United Kingdom, resigning after four months to write 'Why You Don't Need Meat', a top-selling and award-winning book that has changed many people's lives. He has appeared on many TV and radio programmes, including 'Wogan', 'Breakfast Time', 'Six O'Clock News' and 'Today'. He is a founder of Reprieve! (with Chrissie Hynde and Chris Murphy), and is now writing full-time.

1 block of tempeh
2 medium sized onions
Garlic to taste
¼ pint of soya oil
¼ pint of cider vinegar
4 tablespoons of tamari
1 teaspoon of mustard seed
12 whole cloves
12 whole black peppercorns
1 teaspoon of dried herbs (i.e. parsley, thyme, rosemary)

Defrost the tempeh and cut it into one-inch cubes. Chop the onions and garlic finely and put them into a small bowl.

Measure the oil, vinegar and tamari into a pint jug and stir well. Now add the mustard seed, cloves, peppercorns and herbs to the mixture and, again, stir very well.

Arrange the tempeh chunks to cover the bottom of the baking dish. Sprinkle the onion and garlic evenly over them and then pour the marinade sauce over all. Cover the dish and leave the Tempeh Marinade for 6-8 hours. You do not need to stir or attend to it in any way. It does not have to be placed in the fridge.

At the end of this time, bake the Tempeh Marinade for one hour at Gas Mark 5/190°C/375°F. Leaving the cover on the dish will give you a very juicy and light coloured tempeh. If you prefer a crisper texture and a darker colour, uncover the dish after 30 minutes of baking.

While the marinade is baking, cook some brown rice and steam some broccli. Serve the Tempeh Marinade over the rice with the broccoli on the side. This is a very rich dish which improves noticeably when allowed to marinate the full 6-8 hours.

Ample for 2 people.

Beki Bondage

CHESTNUT & MUSHROOM CRUMBLE

Crumble without sugar!

½ lb (227g) onions	
Oregano	
Paprika	
Garlic	
1 lb (455g) chestnuts in season or 1 can Epicure tinned chestnuts (unsweetened purée)	
½ lb (227g) mushrooms	
2 teaspoons Marmite	

Fry onions and garlic in oil (preferably olive) for 5 mins with oregano, paprika and garlic. In same pan add mushrooms and stir until cooked.

Then add chestnuts (cooked and peeled) or chestnut purée. Put this mixture in casserole, add crumble top, and bake for 30 mins.

Beki achieved acclaim and notoriety in the early eighties with punk group Vice Squad. Following the break up of the group she pursued a solo career, which has recently seen her as presenter and star of a new cable TV show 'Live From London'. The promotion of animal rights has always been her primary concern.

A singer who first came to public attention in Willy Russell's 'John, Paul, George, Ringo and Bert', although she had already gained a reputation in the folk clubs. She is now firmly established as an international star, with a considerable number of hit singles, and is well known for a wide number of animal and environmental issues.

Barbara Dickson

COURGETTES À LA POLONAISE

1½ lb (680g) courgettes
4 oz (115g) butter
1 heaped tablespoon flour
½ pint (285ml) milk
Juice of ½ lemon
4 oz (115g) breadcrumbs
4-6 hard-boiled eggs
1 tablespoon chopped parsley
1 tablespoon grated lemon rind
Salt and pepper
Lemon slices and fresh parsley to garnish

Wash, top and tail courgettes and cut into ¼ inch slices. Sauté in a quarter of the butter, turning frequently, until tender.

While that is doing, use another quarter of the butter to make the sauce; melt the butter, then add the flour, and cook for a minute or two. Remove from the heat and gradually add the milk.

Return to heat to thicken, then add lemon juice and seasoning. Simmer gently over a low heat while preparing the polonaise topping. To do this, fry the breadcrumbs in the rest of the butter until golden and crisp.

Finely chop the hard-boiled eggs and add to the breadcrumbs with the parsley and lemon rind: salt and pepper to taste.

To assemble, put the courgettes on a warm serving dish: pour the sauce over and top with the breadcrumb mixture. Garnish with lemon slices and fresh parsley.

Carla Lane

AUBERGINE BAKE

1 large aubergine, cut into thin slices
2 onions, sliced
8 oz (225g) tomatoes, sliced
Seasoning to taste
Good pinch mixed dried herbs
3 oz (85g) Cheddar cheese, grated
Large carton cream
2 oz (55g) chopped nuts

Place half the aubergine slices across the base of a greased ovenproof dish. Top with half the onion, half the tomatoes, seasoning and herbs. Repeat this to use the remaining ingredients.

Top with the cheese, cream and nuts.

Bake at 375°F/190°C/Gas Mark 5 for 15 minutes or until cooked.

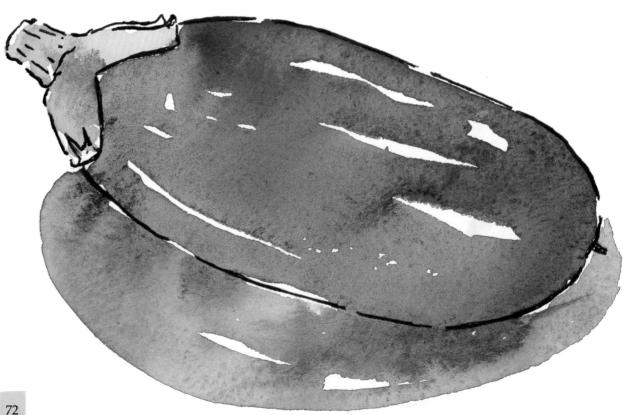

Although her original career was modelling, Susie's face appears regularly on British TV in comedy shows and commercials. She has also made a number of films.

Susie Silvey

VEGETABLE LOAF

2 dressed olives
4 oz (115g) mushrooms
1 oz (30g) margarine/butter
Onion chopped
4 oz (115g) brown rice cooked
4 oz (115g) peas cooked
1 tablespoon tomato purée
1 tablespoon soya sauce
½ teaspoon ground allspice
2 eggs beaten
2 hard-boiled eggs
Salt and pepper

Grease small loaf tin with greaseproof paper. Line tin and brush with oil. Arrange 2 mushrooms down the centre of the tin and olives on each side.

Melt margarine in a saucepan, chop mushrooms and put in pan with onions. Fry gently to soften. Stir in cooked peas, rice, tomato puree, soya sauce, spice and beaten eggs.

When thoroughly mixed put mixture in base of tin. Arrange hard-boiled egs lengthwise in tin and put rest of mixture on top. Press down well.

Put greaseproof paper on top of the mixture and put in a preheated oven 350°F/180°C/ Gas Mark 4 for 35-40 mins until firm to the touch. Leave to go cold in tin. Suggest you serve with jacket potatoes and salad.

Serves 4.

Howard Jones

BROWN RICE RISOTTO

1 medium onion
7 oz (200g) brown rice washed
Approx. ¾ pint (425ml) water
1 rounded teaspoon Marmite
Soya sauce to taste
4 oz (115g) mushrooms
4 oz (115g) sweetcorn/frozen peas
Pinch salt
3 oz (85g) sunflower seeds, dry roasted
½ red pepper

Cook the chopped onion in the oil to soften, wash rice and drain well, add to the onion and cook for several seconds, turning with a fork. Add the hot water in which the Marmite, soya sauce and herbs have been mixed. Bring to the boil and simmer gently.

After 15 mins add the chopped mushrooms and the sweetcorn or peas and simmer for a further 20 to 25 mins until the rice is cooked. Drain if necessary.

Season to taste, top with toasted sunflower seeds and serve. The addition of chopped red pepper gives colour to the dish.

BLACK-EYED BEAN PIE

6 oz (170g) black-eyed beans, soaked overnight	
9 fl oz (250ml) vegetable stock/water	
1 bay leaf	
1 medium onion	
2 carrots	
1 stick celery	
12 oz (340g) boiled potatoes	
1 clove garlic	
1 tablespoon oil	
2 tablespoons tomato purée	
1 teaspoon Marmite	
1 teaspoon mixed herbs	

Drain the beans then put into a pan with clean water. Cook with bay leaf until tender (about 25-30 mins). Chop vegetables, press the garlic, and cook gently together in the oil unti just beginning to soften.

Add purée, drained beans and herbs and mix well together.

Place bean mixture in a greased ovenproof pie dish. Cover with boiled potatoes, thinly sliced, and dot with margarine.

Bake at 400°F/200°C/Gas Mark 6 for 30 mins.

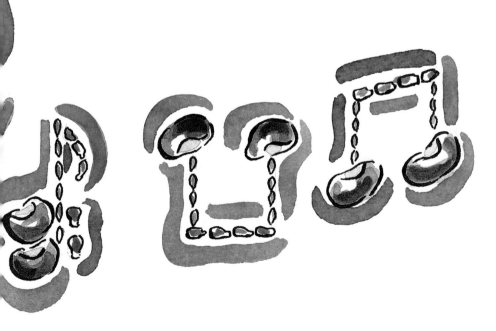

Carol Royle

STUFFED GLOBE ARTICHOKES

4 globe artichokes	
8 oz white bread	
1 small onion	
2 oz butter	
2 lb chopped parsley	
Rind and juice of 1 lemon	
6 oz grated cheese	
Salt and pepper	

Trim top and bottom of artichokes. Remove any damaged outer leaves and topmost leaves to make a cavity for stuffing. Cook artichokes in boiling water until tender and a leaf will come off easily – takes about 45 minutes. Drain artichokes and cut out the inedible hairy 'choke' inside. (I don't do this, but leave it and cut it out when cooked or during the meal. I always find the cutting out of the choke part of the 'fun' ritual of eating artichoke.)

Make stuffing by slicing bread roughly and soaking for a minute or two in warm water. Then squeeze out moisture and break up bread. Chop onion and fry in the butter until transparent but not browned. Add to bread with parsley, lemon rind and juice, most of the cheese, pepper and salt. Pack into artichokes, place them in a buttered casserole and top with remaining cheese.

Bake in a moderate oven, 350°F/Gas Mark 4 for 20 minutes. Serve with melted butter and lemon or Hollandaise Sauce.

Recipe from 'Not Just a Load of Old Lentils' by Rose Elliot

Carol is a very special sort of Thespian: one who can shift from drama to comedy and back again without becoming typecast. Most of her work is for TV and currently she is starring in the TV comedy series 'Life Without George'. However, during her time with the Royal Shakespeare Company she won the London Drama Critics Award for her Ophelia in Michael Pennington's 'Hamlet'. Her support for animal welfare causes is well known.

HOLLANDAISE SAUCE

1 teaspoon lemon juice
1 tablespoon cold water
2 egg yolks (free range)
4 oz butter
Salt and pepper

Mix together lemon juice, water, salt and pepper in top of double saucepan or a bowl set over a pan of hot water – water must not boil.

Beat in egg yolks, then whisk in ¼ of the butter, beating until it has melted and sauce is beginning to thicken. Then add the rest of the butter in three batches; beat well. Add a little more lemon juice if liked, to taste. (I use a hand whisk and I use quite a bit more lemon to taste.) This is a very simple yet lovely recipe for Hollandaise.

Danny Roberts

AUSSIE VEGE BURGERS

½ cup celery (chopped)
½ cup potato (chopped)
½ cup mushrooms (chopped)
½ cup mung beans (sprouted)
½ cup chopped carrots
½ cup chopped onions
½ cup boiled rice (brown)
1 chopped green pepper
1 chopped courgette
1 chopped tomato
1 can kidney beans (pulped)
Garlic, chopped (optional)
Herbs (oregano, basil, mixed herbs, ginger, thyme)
Egg white (free range)
1 cup bread crumbs

Blend it until you can make it into round balls.

Heat in frying pan, or throw on a barbie.

Serves 4.

Danny is one of the fully-rounded professional actors who have emerged from Australia in recent years. Traditionally trained in Shakespearean theatre and classical ballet, he is equally talented in the more modern pursuits of popular music or martial arts. He is best known in Britain for his parts in 'Sons and Daughters' and 'The Sullivans', although these were some time ago. He recently married model Lindsey Neil.

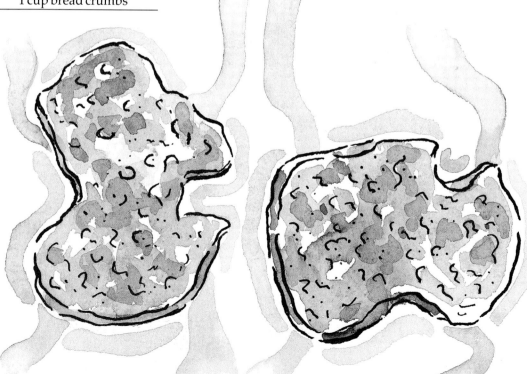

Nerys Hughes came to public notice in Carla Lane's 'Liver Birds', where she played the vegetarian/animal crazy half of the duo. She has played a wide variety of stage and TV roles, including hosting a children's programme with Ralph McTell, and starring in 'The District Nurse'.

Nerys Hughes

SPINACH SURPRISE

3 lb (1.365kg) spinach, chopped
3 pints (1.7 litres) water
Large pinch salt
1½ oz (45g) butter
2 medium onions chopped finely
1 clove garlic (crushed)
6 fl oz (200ml) single cream
5 beaten eggs
½ teaspoon pepper
½ teaspoon grated nutmeg
3 tablespoons finely chopped hazelnuts

Cook spinach, salt and water in pan till tender. Drain all excess liquid. Preheat oven to 350°F/180°C/Gas Mark 4. Grease a deep mould with butter. Melt remaining butter in frypan. Add onion and garlic and fry till onions are transparent but not brown. This is then added to the spinach – mix well.

Beat cream and eggs with salt, pepper and nutmeg. Add this to the spinach mixture. Blend well. Pour into mould. Place in deep roasting tin with enough boiling water to come halfway up side of mould.

Bake in oven for 20-25 mins till risen and set. Remove from oven, sprinkle with nuts and serve at once.

Bon appetit!

It was the death at London Zoo of *Pole Pole*, an elephant with whom they had worked, that inspired the Travers to set up Zoocheck. They have worked tirelessly since for wild animals and their freedom.

Bill Travers

EASTERN PROMISE

1 cup peeled almonds
2 cups of rice
1 red pepper – de-seeded and cut into long, very thin strips
1 small head of celery – cut thinly in small slices
1 clove or piece of chicory – washed and sliced thinly
1 onion very very finely diced or chopped
2 tablespoons of fresh coriander
¼ lb mushrooms
¼ lb frozen peas
2 tablespoons sherry
2 cloves garlic
Finely chopped ginger
1 tablespoon Patak's green garam masala paste
1 cup sunflower or other oil

Gently brown the peeled almonds under a grill.

Take a deep frying pan or wok and put in 1 cup of sunflower seed oil or your favourite cooking oil in which have been crushed 2 cloves of garlic and some very very finely chopped ginger, and 1 tablespoon of Patak's green garam masala curry paste.

To prepare rice take 2 cups Basmati or Patna type rice (not pudding rice). Spread rice on large plate and drawing forward a little at a time take out any discoloured grains. Then wash thoroughly in cold water, drain and put in a large pan. Add 3 cups (same size) of water. Bring to boil. Keep lid on but as soon as steam puffs out turn heat down so steam is just barely visible and set timer for 18 minutes, still do not raise the lid and look, but turn off the heat and leave for 15 minutes to absorb steam. While rice is absorbing this steam, gently heat oil, garlic and ginger; when hot, turn up heat and add celery, chicory, peas, peppers and mushrooms and cook rapidly, tossing the prepared vegetables in the oil for 2-3 minutes. Then add the onion, coriander and garam masala paste (which has been thinned by mixing a tablespoon of sunflower oil)

and cook moving all the ingredients about in the hot oil for a further 2 minutes. Leave covered on minimum heat.

The rice has now been standing for 15 minutes so the steam will have been absorbed. It should be stirred to break it up and mixed into the vegetables in a large deep frying pan or wok.

Now add 2 tablespoons of sherry and sprinkle on the roasted almonds. Cover and turn off heat.

I like to eat this with a nice chilled medium dry fruity wine. Take care not to overcook the vegetables. They should not be mushy.

There is a variation if you are an egg-eating vegetarian like me which I can thoroughly recommend. While the rice is absorbing the steam make a four free-range egg plain omelette and cut this into decorative strips. Add it in layers attractively after adding the sherry but before adding the toasted almonds. Remember you have to move quickly so as not to let the omelette cool, and for heaven's sake eat it while it is still hot!

Serves 4

Paul Weller

Nut Roast à la Weller

2 oz (55g) TVP mince beef flavour hydrated in water

4 oz (115g) chopped cashew nuts (unsalted)

1 tablespoon margarine

1 small onion

Vegetarian gravy

½ teaspoon garlic powder

Salt and pepper

Put the TVP and water into a saucepan, cook until soft. In another pan, heat the margarine. Put in chopped onion and cook until the onion is soft and brown. Add ½ teaspoon of garlic powder.

Add the cooked TVP (once drained), and season with salt and pepper. Add chopped/grated nuts and stir well. Then add vegetarian gravy until mixture is bound together but not too runny.

When mixture is hot put it into an ovenproof dish and bake at 400°F/200°C/Gas Mark 6 for 40 minutes.

This is great as a Sunday dinner with roast potatoes, vegetables and mint sauce.

Serves 2.

Brigid Brophy

STUFFED
(but not banally with rice)
PEPPERS

Author of some of the best and most experimental novels published since the war, as well as the driving force behind Public Lending Right, Brigid Brophy is a committed Vegan and takes an uncompromising stance on the abuse of animals.

6 small green or red sweet peppers
4 oz (115g) mushrooms
3 onions, sliced
Olive oil
2 oz (55g) celery leaves
2 oz (55g) parsley
2 large grated carrots
3 crushed cloves of garlic
1 lemon
1 teaspoon chopped dill
Salt and pepper

Cut the tops off the peppers, remove the stalks, seeds and pith, and put the tops aside. Gently fry the mushrooms and the onions in the olive oil until they are soft and have released their liquids.

Chop the celery leaves and the parsley and mix them with the carrots in the bowl. Add the mushrooms and the onions to the carrot mixture, with the remaining oil and vegetable liquids, the garlic, lemon zest, dill and seasoning. Mix well together.

Stuff the peppers with the filling, place them in a saucepan and put their tops back on. Squeeze the juice from the lemon over them and pour in enough water to surround them half-way up their sides.

Let them simmer gently for 45 minutes, when they can be picked out with a perforated spoon and left to drain for a moment before serving. The liquid that is left makes a good basic stock for soups.

If you have men who will exclude any of God's creatures from the shelter of compassion and pity, you will have men who will deal likewise with their fellow men.

JESUS

SWEETS
& BAKED
THINGS

Country Joe McDonald

CORN BREAD

My favourite way to eat this is not with salt and pepper and butter but with vinegar and Louisiana hot sauce. Drink milk with this meal. There you have a traditional working class American veg meal.

1 cup of corn meal (fine or coarse ground)
1 cup of white flour (if you are really a nutrition nut just use all corn meal but it will not be very light in the end)
2-4 tablespoons of sweetening: honey, brown sugar, etc.
1 tablespoon of baking powder
1 teaspoon salt
¾ cup of soft vegetable shortening/margarine
1 or 2 eggs depending on how much cholesterol you want in your diet
1 cup of milk (or a little less if you used honey)

Preheat oven to 400°F/200°C/Gas Mark 6. *It is very important* to use a cast iron pan for corn bread and you *must preheat* the pan in the oven at the same time as the oven. While you are waiting blend all the ingredients together in a bowl, and mix well.

When the pan and oven are hot take the pan out and grease the side and bottom with butter, then pour in the mixture. Now cook for 20-25 minutes. Remove from oven and flip it out of the pan on to a tea-towel and on to a plate. Keep covered with a towel for a few minutes to keep in the heat and make sure it is cooked well.

Serve the corn bread hot with whatever bread topping you like; jam, jelly, butter, margarine, etc, or just plain like cake.

Country Joe adds: I eat corn bread with greens.

There are lots of leaves called greens; swiss chard, beetroot tops, turnip tops, collard greens, even dandelion leaves; all are dark green and vary from sweet like spinach to tart. Cook one kind or mix them. But cook them much longer than spinach. Boil for 20-30 minutes (while the corn bread is cooking).

Serve hot.

A third generation political activist, Joe McDonald's song 'Feel like I'm a fixin to die rag' was the anthem of those who eventually brought about the end of the Vietnam war. He was himself a Vietnam veteran, and continues to work with support groups for those still gripped by the horrors of that conflict. Country Joe and the Fish's LP 'Electric Music for the Mind and Body' was the definitive album of the psychedelic movement. Since that group's demise, Country Joe has pursued a solo career, exploring just about all forms of popular music. During the last fifteen years he has been the most consistent artist with regard to animal and environmental issues.

His recorded works on these subjects were compiled on the first Animal Rights LP to be issued, 'Animal Tracks', released by Animus Records in 1983.

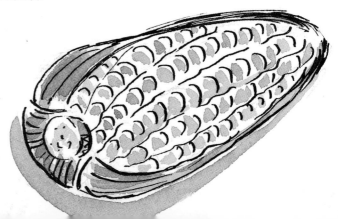

Kate Bush

GRANARY BREAD

I thought it might be nice to include a recipe for good old home-made bread, not only good nutrition wise, but also I feel the actual process of making bread is very therapeutic.

Her debut album, 'The Kick Inside' the most refreshing release of the 1970, showed an exceptional promise which has come to fruition over the last decade. The complete artist for the video age, because of her many talents – mime, dance, performance, and a creative imagination which has a visual as well as an aural aspect. Kate Bush has taken a public stand on eating animals, native peoples' rights and Third World issues.

Just over 3 lb (1.4kg) granary flour
1 oz (30g) margarine
approx. 1½ pint (855ml) tepid water
1½ oz (45g) yeast
pinch of salt
½ teaspoon honey

Put the flour into a bowl and rub in the margarine so that it is evenly distributed.

Take a cupful of water from the 1½ pints and stir in the yeast and honey so that both are completely dissolved. Make a hole in the centre of the flour and add the dissolved yeast, then the rest of the water. Add the salt.

Mix to make a dough, then knead this for a few minutes so that it is smooth and free from lumps. Set aside in a warm place for 30 minutes.

Divide the dough into three and form loaf shapes. Put them into bread bins. (For rolls shape into rounds approximately 2" across and place on baking trays.) Leave them to rise for 35 minutes. Place in a hot oven and cook for 35-40 minutes. (Rolls need only 10-20 minutes, depending on crispness desired.)

To tell if bread is cooked, tap it with your knuckles – it should sound hollow. Place on a wire rack to cook – for a softer centred loaf, cover bread with a clean tea-towel whilst it is cooling.

Nanette Newman

THREE MELON SALAD

1 watermelon
1 honeydew melon
1 charentais melon
Lemon balm or pineapple mint (if you have it)
Medium tin lychees, drained

Cut a slice off the top of the watermelon to make a lid. Scoop out all the flesh and cut it into chunks, discarding the seeds. Put the watermelon flesh into a bowl. Halve the honeydew, discard the seeds, then scoop out the flesh and mix with the watermelon. Do the same with the charentais. (You can use a melon baller for this.)

Add the sprigs of lemon balm or mint and the lychees to the melon mixture. Fill the watermelon shell with the melon and wrap it securely in a couple of thicknesses of cling film.

Pack the melon in plenty of ice or a cold fridge. Serve very cold.

Serves 6 to 9

Nanette Newman has been leading lady for an impressive number of quality British films, including 'The L-Shaped Room', 'The League of Gentlemen' and 'The Whisperers'. Some of her best performances have been in films directed by her husband, Bryan Forbes. More recently, she has become recognised as a star of light comedy in TV sit-coms, and is a popular author and compiler of children's books. She is an inventive cook, and the recipes here are taken from her 'Summer Cookbook' and reproduced by kind permission of Bryan Forbes Ltd.

CLASSIC SUMMER PUDDING

2½ lb (1.135kg) fruit, including redcurrants and blackcurrants, blackberries and raspberries
6 oz (170g) caster sugar
Grated rind of 1 lemon
4 tablespoons port
1 small wholemeal loaf (or white if you prefer)
Whole fruit to decorate
Whipped cream to serve

Put the currants and any other fruit which needs cooking in a saucepan with the sugar, fruit rinds and juice. Poach gently until the juice runs and the fruit is softened. (You can also use strawberries, rhubarb, cherries, peaches and plums in summer pudding.)

Mix all the types of fruit together and stir in the port. Cut the crusts off the bread and slice it fairly thinly. Line a 1.15 litre/2 pint pudding basin with the bread, then put the fruit in and top with more bread. Cover and weight down, and chill for several hours. Reserve any remaining fruit to pour over the pudding when it is turned out or whip the juice into double cream until thick.

Ease the blade of a palette knife between the pudding and the basin to loosen the pudding, then invert it on to a serving dish and pour over any reserved juice. Surround the pudding with lots of whole fruit – currants and soft fruit.

Serve with whipped cream.

Serves 4 to 6.

Lindsey Neil

TOFU LEMON FLAN

FOR FLAN:
8 oz (225g) vegan digestive biscuits
4 oz (115g) vegan margarine, melted

FOR FILLING:
6 tablespoons golden or maple syrup
1 oz (30g) cornflour
¾ pint (425ml) water
8 oz (225g) tofu
6 tablespoons lemon juice
1 tablespoon grated lemon rind
Green and black grapes

Crumble the biscuits and mix with the margarine. Use the mixture to line a medium-sized flan ring placed on a baking sheet. Set aside.

Put the syrup, cornflour and water into a saucepan. Heat gently, stirring until the sauce thickens.

Mash the tofu well and combine with the lemon juice and rind (this can be done in a blender). Add this mixture to the saucepan, stir and cook gently a few minutes more, then set aside to cool slightly.

Pour mixture into prepared flan case, top with the grapes arranged in circles (these can be halved). Chill the flan until it sets firm.

Ex Benny Hill's Angel and popular model, Lindsey was born into an army family and, during a childhood spent in Asia, developed an affinity with the abundant wildlife there. Her early years seem to have determined the restless pattern of her life. After a recent spell in Australia, she and her dog Cain are now in Los Angeles pursuing a career in films.

COCONUT CREAM DESSERT

¾ pint (425ml) coconut milk
2 oz (55g) raw cane sugar
2 oz (55g) arrowroot
Kiwi fruit or banana to decorate

The coconut milk can be made from a block of creamed coconut, or by blending fresh coconut with water and straining off the milk. Put the milk into a heavy-based saucepan with the sugar and arrowroot.

Cook over a medium heat, stirring continually, until the mixture thickens to a cream. Do not let it boil. Divide the cream between four bowls, cool first, and then chill. Just before serving decorate each bowl with thin slices of kiwi fruit or banana (if using banana, brush the fruit with lemon juice first so it doesn't go brown).

This sauce can be made thicker by using a little more arrowroot. It is then ideal as a filling for a sweet flan.

Joanna Lumley

AMAZING PUDDING

½ pint (285ml) goat or sheep yoghurt
½ pint (285ml) really thick double cream
2 huge spoonfuls of dark brown sugar

Stir the yoghurt and cream together gently and put into a fairly shallow dish. Sprinkle liberally with sugar and put in the fridge for a couple of hours.

Serve in glasses with langues de chat biscuits (or any kind of fiddly pretty little biscuit). Perfect on its own, or with something dull that needs a delicious splodge on top.

Rita Tushingham

RITA'S ENGLISH TRIFLE

There are a number of films which captured the mood and feel of the sixties and it seems as if Rita Tushingham appeared in all of them – films like 'A Taste of Honey', 'The Knack' and 'Georgie Girl'. Based in Toronto, Rita has continued her film career with the occasional foray into British television in Carla Lane's 'No Strings' and 'Bread'. Along with Carla and Linda McCartney she is a founder of Animaline. Rita tells us that this recipe was a prize winner in Canada.

2 packages sponge cake (equivalent 1 layer tin size)
1 tin raspberries with juice
2 bananas
1 small tin fruit cocktail (drained and chopped)
Raspberry jam (seedless)
Sherry
1/2 cups whipping cream
1 pint of milk
3 tablespoons custard powder
6 teaspoons sugar or to taste

Cut sponge cake in half and spread with raspberry jam. Break into pieces and place in large bowl. Pour on tin of raspberries and fruit cocktail. Slice bananas thinly and place on top. Liberally lace with sherry – don't be mean when sprinkling it.

Cover and refrigerate overnight.

Next day – Make custard mixture with custard powder. Pour over top of cake mixture (you don't need to cool it first). Let set again in refrigerator for about 2 hours. When set, whip the cream spreading over the top and garnish with nuts such as slivered almonds and fresh strawberries or raspberries. Use a glass bowl or a colourful patterned one if possible.

Jenny Beavan

JENNY'S PUDDING

This is an easy, but elegant, dinner party pudding. A variation is to substitute the wine and lemon juice for 2 tablespoons orange liqueur plus the juice and finely grated rind of an orange, making an Orange Sabayon – equally delicious!

2 free-range eggs
4 oz sugar
¼ litre dry white wine
1 teaspoon cornflour
2 dessertspoons lemon juice

Beat the eggs and sugar together in a pan, then whisk in the wine, cornflour and lemon juice.

When thoroughly whisked, cook over a slow heat, beating all the time until thickened. Remove from heat, but continue beating for another minute.

Pour into glasses. I usually serve Amaretti biscuits with this pudding.

Serves 4.

One of our most successful film costume designers, Jenny Beavan has been nominated three times for an Oscar, and once for the British Academy award – winning both in 1986 for her work on Merchant Ivory's 'A Room With A View'. Jenny grew up in a family interested in health food and alternative medicine, and is bringing up her daughter Caitlin on the same lines.

Carla Lane

DOG BISCUITS

3 lb (1.4kg) wholemeal flour
½ lb (225g) margarine
1½ tablespoon salt
spoonful of yeast extract

Rub fat into flour and salt. Dissolve yeast extract in a little hot water. Make up to 1½ pts.

Mix into flour to make a dough.

Roll out to ¼" thick. Cut into shapes. Put onto baking tray. Bake at 350°F/180°C/Gas Mark 4 for 45 minutes.

When cold, store in an airtight tin.